DEAR NOLITA

The Evolution of an Addict's Son

© WESLEY HAWKINS 2019

DISCLAIMER

This is the past as I remember it.

To maintain the privacy of people still living, in some instances I have changed the names of individuals and places, and identifying characteristics and details such as physical properties, dates, and places of residence.

This is for all of you who feel like there's no way out.

FOREWORD

So many of us from the hood love the street. But we don't realize that the streets don't love us back. The streets are our homes. They're also where young men, women, kids, and elders are being robbed, beat, and killed every day.

The streets are where you go to use or sell drugs. Where you see neighbors dying from dope, skinny because they can't afford or remember to eat. The streets are where families are broken and hearts are ripped apart.

The streets are where darkness lives. Yet we are taught to admire them.

I'm from the streets of Baltimore. I've seen the worst of the worst and felt some of the heaviest pain. The streets took my childhood. The streets took my mother, and then her life. The streets took my father, and my younger brother's father. I knew homelessness, crack dens, foster care.

I learned to succeed on the streets. I loved them when I was younger. I ran blocks, bought sports cars, had status. I was taught that the streets were the place to be.

But looking back, my childhood and that street life was so ugly I'm thankful and blessed to be alive today. I could easily have died. Or worse. I could've killed somebody.

I had to work hard to learn how to love myself. The streets are never gonna teach you that. They depend on you hating yourself, you see. On you not caring if you're being harmed, or doing harm.

Self-love is what I teach. It is the regard for your own well-being and happiness. It means you take care of yourself - not caring if that's 'cool' or easy.

You have to learn to love yourself first before you can properly love anyone or anything else. You can't care for a family, a child, if you don't care for yourself.

If you don't love yourself, you'll always be trying to fill that hole inside you. That's why so many of our people are on drugs, dying and killing each other. That's what happened to my mother.

When you love yourself, you won't let people treat you badly. You won't treat yourself bad, either. You won't tolerate the things that harm you or other people.

You won't treat others bad 'cause you won't have that hole inside yourself. You won't need to fill it up by putting yourself above other people.

It's a long road to get there. So long if you're born in the streets, born knowing nothing but hustling and homelessness, surrounded by people who gave up hope.

But if I can get there, so can you.

This book is the story of how I did it. I'm sharing it in hopes that it might help you.

CONTENTS

MARY

I've got to the point that I wish I had wings
I'd stand on my tippy toes, spread my wings and fly away
You'd see me glide from city to city tryna find my way
I would speak for all the people in pain,
This what they say –

Mary's father was the definition of savage. He and his brothers ran their hood like a country with borders. Anybody they didn't like had better stay away. Violence was the only way they knew to feel strong, in control.

Mary's spirit was molded by her father's trauma, but her heart was cast in gold. She was born sharin', carin', brown eyes sparklin', happy to help. You need those dishes done? You need that floor swept? If you needed money and she had any, she'd lend it to you.

A lot of people took advantage of Mary that way - borrowing and borrowing, and never paying back. But this chapter ain't about that.

This chapter is about Mary and her father.

Her father was a bully. You looked at him the wrong way,

he'd beat it out of you. Get all up in your face to try to scare you, and that was a warning. Respect was important to him, and he didn't see the difference between respect and fear. Fear was easier to get. So he collected a lot of it.

Mary got some of that trait from him. Which could be kind of hilarious, because she was also 4'11" and ninety pounds.

Mary learned a lot of things from her daddy. Too many things.

Her father ruled his roost like a warlord. The family home, and everything in it, was his. Including the women. *All* the women.

Mary knew what sex was by age eleven because of her dad. He'd come into her room at night, and her sister's room too. Her sister bore a child by her father - so with Mary, he took precautions. He didn't want any more babies - said he'd had enough of kids for one lifetime. So he only raped his daughter in other forbidden places.

That meant when she came down pregnant, he knew it wasn't his. He knew she'd cheated on him.

My grandpa was a young man, then. A teenager, like Mary. He loved her. It's too bad I didn't get to meet him.

Back then Mary was this tiny girl from the worst part of town who was sweet as a saint when she was in her right mind, mean as the devil when she wasn't.

That's what her father did to her - what happens to a lot of girls who are abused. Their bodies scream *no, no,* but there ain't a damn thing they can do about it. Forever and for the rest of their lives, sometimes their minds and bodies just start screaming *no!* and they fight, and they hate, and they'll tear to shreds anybody who's standing near 'em because they couldn't do that to their daddies. They depended on their daddies to survive.

My grandpa saw who Mary wanted to be. Who she was when she wasn't scared. He saw this girl who wanted to make the whole world shine, who couldn't bear to see anybody having any sort of problem. He saw this girl who couldn't be happy unless everybody was happy, who sometimes suddenly got spitting scared and fighting mad, small hands ballin' up into fists, prepared to fight, and even she didn't know why.

You might expect their story to have an unhappy ending. It does, but not the kind you're thinking. Mary came down pregnant with my mother when my grandpa was seventeen, and he immediately proposed to her.

He didn't get to marry her right away. His parents insisted that he finish high school, go to college, start a career. He was a smart man, and more important, he was disciplined. His parents said he could've been anything. And they were right.

My grandpa struck a compromise with them: he'd finish high school, marry Mary, and then join the Marines. The Marines could give him a career as prestigious as any. More prestigious than most, if he stuck with them. And he could start making money to support Mary and the baby right away. He did it all: graduated, got accepted by the Marines, started planning the wedding.

On Mary's end, things weren't going so well.

Her jealous Daddy didn't like her cheating on him. I imagine old street lights filtering through curtains as she told him, or as he guessed. I imagine his eyes bulging, veins pulsing in his temples, spit flying as he heard the news.

I wonder: Did he hit his pregnant daughter?

Did her mother stop him from hitting her?

Did her mother do anything at all?

If something had gone different, somewhere along the line, things might have been different for all of us. The effects of cruelty ripple through time, cascade down the generations, until someone has the strength to stop them. The traumatic abuse Mary endured determined the course of my mother's life, and mine. One could speculate who's cruelty shaped my great-grandfather's life, and all the lives before that.

At some point, my family was enslaved. They'd have been treated as property, dominated through brute force. Maybe my great-great-great-grandad learned that domination was power. Maybe he learned to do the same to his women, and taught his son, who taught his son, and so on until we got to Mary's dad.

We all learn what power is from somewhere, maybe from plantations, from the people who had power over us when we were children. We all learn from our parents, and that's how trauma cascades, stopping only in those rare, bright moments when we stop and self-reflect.

Those bright moments are happening more and more often, now.

Mary's parents kicked her out, is the long and short of it. They put their pregnant teenage daughter out on the street. But Mary was lucky: her lover and his family were good people, upstanding people, in the Christly sense, not the holier-than-thou sort of way.

They took her in, and from then on it was like Mary was one of their own children.

With the help of his family, my grandpa graduated, married Mary, passed the Marine's aptitude tests with flying colors. They're an example of how kindness ripples too. Kindness and truama, both always rippling out through time and space. Which one wins is down to the choices we make every day.

Mary gave birth to a beautiful baby girl - my mother, Nolita. It was a fairytale come true. The princess and the knight in shining armor, their daughter raised in a castle by the sea. My mother's family moved around Marine bases with Tony's deployments, and from the outside, they were the model military family.

But there's a lot of things the fairy tales don't tell us.

The scars Mary's dad left on her weren't fading. Scars like those often don't just disappear. It takes therapy, effort, and self-knowledge. The 1970s weren't exactly huge on any of those things.

Mary didn't get any therapy.

Instead, she loved her baby girl the only way she knew how. Nolita, with her mother's delicate bones and her father's proud bearing, became Mary's best buddy. Her daughter was her main gal pal, her constant companion.

Sounds sweet, right?

It wasn't.

When her husband wasn't around, Mary's favorite thing to do was party. Sex, drugs, and drinks. Quiet moments sent her back to nights in her bedroom, to her daddy coming in. To what should have been the safest place in the world for her, but wasn't.

So she picked noise. Loud talking and loud music, and whatever drugs she could get. Mary drank like a fish; a normal part of socializing in the seventies, so nobody called her an "alcoholic." As long as she had cleaned herself up and cleaned the house by the time Tony got home, she was good.

Mary gave Tony three children. Nolita, the oldest; Tony Jr., and Antoinette. By the time Nolita was ten years old, she had siblings ages 5 and 6, both with special needs that required Mary's constant attention.

She also had an adult woman's walk, swaying hips and a seductive smile learned from long years spent studying Mary and her friends. Mary didn't seem to notice, or didn't care. She was busy socializing and entertaining. She'd never made much time for her daughter to play with other children. She just brought her daughter to play with her grown women friends.

There came one morning when Mary became, suddenly, afraid. Tony had said that he needed to go to a dinner in the evening, a military dinner with the men he worked for.

Some part of Mary, deep down, felt that she hadn't seen him much lately. She felt that, worn down by childcare, she must not have been enough fun for Tony anymore. Wouldn't he stay tonight? Couldn't he stay?

No. He'd made a commitment. And he was running late.

Mary lost it. She started swinging at him. He put his hands on her shoulders, each arm six inches longer than hers, and held her at bay. She reached for him with flailing claws and fists. He waited.

Tony had always been patient. His siblings said they'd never seen him talk back to his parents. He'd talked back to his mother, just once - then run out of the house, horrified by what he'd done.

"Baby," he said, looking at the watch where it sat on his wrist, being tossed around by her flailing. "Baby, I'm gonna be late."

Mary kept coming.

"Baby, come on. *Please.*"

Mary let out a shriek of despair. She was finally spent. In a few hours, Tony knew, his wife would find her head again. He would make it up to her, then.

But in the meantime, he was running late.

The military doesn't like lateness. Tony's commitment to showing up on time helped him rise through the ranks. He was always disciplined, never angry. If ever anger creased his smooth, wise face, he left to be alone until he'd cooled down. He was patient, gentle, kind.

And he was never, never late.

So Tony drove to the house of a new recruit, to give the soldier a lift.

During the ride, he was driving too fast as he rounded a sharp turn in the road.

And found himself staring at the headlights of another car.

Tony yanked the wheel, hard, to the right. The old woman who had been driving down the middle of a two-lane road passed by, safe.

Tony's car rolled.

Tony saw the tree coming. He saw that it would come through the windshield and destroy everything above the dashboard.

He reached over, unbuckled his recruit's seatbelt, and shoved the younger man down, out of harm's way.

And as he used his body weight to hold the recruit down in safety, the tree took Tony's head off.

Mary was taken care of, for a little while, on Tony's benefits. But she wasn't ever quite right in the head again.

She had been told, growing up, that everything was her fault. In a family like her dad's, like her uncles', you blame the only thing that can't hit back. Usually, that's the kids. It is especially the tiny, frail girl who cowers when her father shouts. *'Why did you make me do that?'*

That self-blame was where Mary's violence came from. The weight of feeling responsible for every bad thing that had ever happened to *anyone* hung over her like an atom bomb. Sometimes, without warning, it'd blow up.

She'd been told by family her whole life that she was bad and shameful. That she was the cause of all things bad. Tony's death only made it worse. Made her explosions more frequent, more destructive.

Maybe that explains what happened to my mother.

BEAUTIFUL NOLITA

I can't wait until I make it
Na homie I ain't yet made it
It's just a matter of time
You better place your bets
I'm rolling sevens in this game

Mary was my grandmother. Nolita was my mother. I tell this part, not from what I remember, but from what others have told me. In this way, I try to understand my mother.

Nolita was practically born in makeup and a designer dress. She had her mother's glamor and her father's good looks and charm. She had brown eyes that could inflict love or terror and a smile that could make a man need her the way he needed oxygen. She learned to rely on these things early.

Being a military kid meant that Nolita's enrollment in school was sketchy at best. Her absences were only sometimes noticed, and it was usually assumed that there was a reason for them. Her daddy was, after all, the biggest, most handsome, upstanding man in the toughest, most prestigious branch of the military. If Nolita wasn't in school, there had to be a good reason.

The reason, usually, was that her mother was taking her to parties.

By six years old, Nolita could explain sex better than most adults. She seemed to think sex was a normal thing to do at parties. She had seen grown-ups do it loads of times. At six she wanted to be a party girl, a femme fatale, a seductress - just like her mother.

And like her father, Nolita was good at everything she tried.

She studied fashion the way other girls studied the alphabet, danced the way adult women danced, and she spoke their language with a young sophisticated tongue. Her mother never told Nolita she was too young for anything. Not until it was too late. Not until some familiar grown men had gotten to her, and fucked her up for life.

Nolita had an aunt and mother figure named Patty. She was Tony's little sister. Patty was ten years older than Nolita, and raised by the same parents who raised strong, upstanding Tony. Patty tried to help.

She took Nolita out for bike rides, and to the park. She signed her up for gymnastics and soccer. She did everything she could to help Nolita experience a childhood . To help her have some time in her life when no one wanted anything from her.

But she also listened. She heard Nolita describe sex, seduction, and adult social politics. How you couldn't trust people. How they always wanted something from you. How you could use your body to get things from men. From a girl too young to know who she was. Patty worried that she'd become a clone of her mother's friends - women with long lashes and short skirts, before she ever got to be Nolita.

By the time Nolita turned 11, Patty knew that she was having sex. She was still one of the "cool kids" - an elder who visited from the mysterious realm called "college." So the children still talked in front of her. One afternoon she listened in as Nolita entertained friends.

"It feels like having a broomstick shoved up in you," one child said with a curious stare. "Doesn't it, Nolita?"

Nolita smiled with her glossed lips and shadowed eyes. The kind of smile only a much older woman should have. She stared back into memories too soon familiar. "Not," she said coyly, "if you do it right."

Patty kept silent. She knew that if she got upset, Nolita would never be honest with her again.

"Have you done it with boys, Nolita?" Patty asked, faking curiosity.

"Yeah," Nolita said, with fake humility. "Lots of them. Boys will give you anything you want, if you give them what they want." She spoke with swag and confidence, not showing the guilt that hid behind it .

Patty felt the pit of her stomach drop out. Her eyes fought back tears as she listened.

"But you can't tell my ma, Aunt Patty, okay? She would be so mad." Nolita had already perfected the beguiling look, the batting of the eyelashes.

"Okay," Patty said, knowing this was a promise that she would have to break.

☆☆☆

"You have to take your daughter to the doctor," Patty said. "You have to get her on birth control."

Mary grew bitter with age. There was a frightening hardness in her eyes, in the lines of her face. With two children who could not care for themselves, she had no time or energy for her oldest daughter.

"Why should she need birth control?" Mary demanded. "The girl is eleven years old!"

"She's sexually active, Mary."

Mary stopped. It must have been her father's training that welled up in her then. She turned, looked up at Patty. Met her eyes with a stone face that was terrifying, even on her tiny body.

"If that slut is having sex," Mary said, "it's not my problem."

Patty wanted to scream that it was her problem, that Nolita was her child. She wanted to pull her by the heart and drag her to her daughter's pain.

Instead, she went to the drug store and bought Nolita condoms.

☆☆☆

The next time Patty saw Nolita, Nolita would not speak to her. She looked at her sidelong, a glint of frightening anger in her eyes. Her mother's anger. Her eyes said *something bad happened to me because of you.*

"Hi Nono," Patty said, soft enough to show that she saw the

difference. Cheerful enough to say she expected things were fine anyway.

Nolita turned her head away. Her hair, Patty noticed, was immaculately styled. The style made Nolita, and her budding curves, look much older than she was.

"I asked your ma to get you some medicine," Patty tried, stopping, looking down at Nolita.

"I ain't sick," Nolita said.

"Well then...take these anyway." Patty glanced up and down the long hallway to make sure no one was watching them before she pulled the condoms out.

"I don't need 'em," Nolita said, batting her hand away. The condoms hit the floor, and Patty scrambled to pick them up.

"Nolita...you do."

Nolita finally turned to look at Patty, then, meeting her eye. In Nolita's eyes, Patty saw Mary's cold rage. The look that came from knowing something terrible had happened, and no one did anything about it.

"Why don't you mind your own goddamn business?" Nolita asked, turning her eyes away from Patty, like Patty wasn't even there.

✰✰✰

Since Tony's death, Mary enlisted help from her support system as she raised three kids while working to pay the bills. Patty often brought Mary groceries to help lift her burden. She would often visit Mary and as time went on, Party Girl Mary had vanished. There was no time anymore.

On this particular day as Patty visited, something seemed off. She slowly entered the home, her thoughts moving faster than her feet as she crept through towards the back.

There she found what her eyes could never forget. Patty's gaze slithered from the bottom of Nolita's feet,oddly facing the ceiling up her brown legs to the bend of her knee as she knelt at the alter of the unconscionable. Patty's eyes quickly shifted to the crumpled pants and hanging belt shrowded on the the floor.

The sin itself strangled her tongue.

Dispair, disgust and pain creeped up her throat like cement. A tearing paper bag broke the silence as thuds of vegetables and fruit hit the carpet.

Nolita's shame flashed across her face as she bolted from the room and then out of the house.

The uncle stood, naked from the waist down, looking at Patty.

"You understand," he said, "why we can't tell anybody about this."

"We? Who's *we?*"

"It'll come back on Mary, if you do. On Tony's reputation."

"Tony ain't got nothing to do with this!"

His belt jingled as he straightened his pants, as he turned to leave.

"Don't worry about it," a dismissive shrug hung on his shoulders. "It won't happen anymore, if that'll make you feel better."

In her mind, Patty leapt across the room ensnaring him in her grip, squeezing his eyes until blood and membrane were in her hands. She worked up enough breath to yell, "Get *out!*" as he strolled slowly, carelessly out of view. Her feet were lead on the floor as if one step would unravel the earth. She saw her little girl disappear. She wanted to disappear. She wanted the world to disappear.

☆☆☆

I'd like to say the family sided with Patty. But they didn't. Patty learned real quick why so many abuse victims don't talk.

"You can't do that to this family," Mary said. "Everybody's going to ask why I let him be alone with her!"

"Think of Tony's reputation," a grandma pleaded. "He worked hard to be respected. Don't make people think about this when they hear Tony's name."

Patty steeled herself, and told anyway. The crime committed against Nolita was too much to ignore.

A psychology student, Patty knew the laws, and she knew what to do. She called social services for help, for Nolita's protection.

They asked for evidence.

What passed for an investigation in the 1980s, regarding the alleged rape of a black female child, was a series of interviews with her family. It involved no physical examination of Nolita; and from the way the interviewers looked at Nolita, Patty could see what they thought: *that eleven-year-old is a slut, anyway.*

No charges were filed. No protective action was taken. Everything continued as it was.

Except Nolita stopped talking to Patty.

☆☆☆

By thirteen, Nolita slept around. Gorgeous by anyone's standards, she learned fast to attract men with money.

The game was played on the party scene, where Nolita excelled. She followed her mother's example of escaping into sex and drink.

While her mother worked, Nolita had free reign of the streets. School held no attraction for her. The laws of physics were not as important as the laws of the streets. When she did go, she often scowled, shouted, and lashed out at teachers who told her what rules she must follow. What had rules ever done to keep her safe?

By her fourteenth birthday, Nolita's belly swelled round with child. With me.

The announcement made Mary mad. Like her father before her, she screamed, eyes bulging, voice hoarse with shouting: "*I ain't raisin' no more babies!*"

Patty's family took Nolita in, like they'd taken Mary before her.

For a while, it seemed like things were gonna be okay.

☆☆☆

Family says that for the first three years of my life, I was Nolita's little angel. She treasured me, kept me safe and warm and loved. Maybe that's why I loved her so much, even after all the things she did later. Maybe part of me remembered. Maybe the memories were seared into the fabric of my heart.

One story that the family loves to tell is how Nolita would dress me up. My mother always had a passion for fashion, for looking glamorous. She would dress both of us up until we looked like a magazine centerfold, some hip hop black Madonna and Child with perfect ringlets, gold bling and me in frilly royal outfits that made me look like a prince.

My mother and I were the envy of the town, with the way she took care of me. Everybody assumed that if we looked that good, she must make good choices. That she was herself a child only, somehow, made us cuter.

But Nolita had her own ideas about life. To my mother, school was a waste of time. She struggled to focus, struggled to behave, got yelled at by the teachers constantly. Looking back, it's possible that my mother and her mother both had some kind of mental illness.

But almost nobody got diagnosed with mental illness in the 1980s. What the teachers and principals knew was that she was a black girl who dressed too sexy, who already had a kid at fourteen, who skipped class constantly and didn't do her homework. As far as they were concerned, she was a lost cause.

Nolita figured, if they were gonna treat her like that, why go?

School wasn't the way that girls got up in the world, on the streets of West Baltimore in the 1980s. My mother saw one way to get wealth and status, and that was by wooing men with money.

☆☆☆

Nolita liked men with deep pockets. She was drawn to the allure of glamour and success. Problem was, on the streets of West Baltimore, men with money were men who sold drugs.

When crack hit the streets, it didn't take long for it to transform the community. Here was something so addictive people would kill to get more after just a few hits. Here was something that a single hustler could get most of his neighborhood hooked on in the span of a couple weeks.

And once they were hooked, customers would come back twitching. Fidgeting. Losing weight from spending cash on crack instead of food. They would do *anything* to get more cash to buy more crack.

If you were the hustler they gave the cash to, life was good.

Once they were addicted, folks would pay for crack before they'd pay for medicine. Folks could be homeless and still give their hustler every cent they could get their hands on, they would turn to crime to pay when they couldn't keep a job anymore. Trading sex for money became normal, as did muggings, robberies, and all manner of theft.

This made the hustlers the new lords of the ghetto. Just like the feudal lords of old taxed their starving peasants, the hustlers took every cent that anybody wanted to spend on crack. Which, pretty soon, was *all* of it.

And just like the old lords, they soon began to feel pretty good about their success. If they spent some of their money on churches, on mortgages for old ladies, on tuition for local kids - that made it all okay, right? Pretty soon, the local hustler was the local crime lord and the local social services all in one.

A skilled kingpin could bring in tens of thousands a week. Some of it went to charity, and some went to by flaunting their success in the most showy, elaborate ways possible.

Using the finest bling to buy the finest women was a major way of showing off success. If you were a woman with the right shape, the right attitude, that high-class style, hustlers would buy you diamonds, cars, designer clothes that told everybody empirically that you were the baddest bitch on the block.

Just like for rich white folks, it wasn't even about enjoying the luxuries. It was about what the luxuries proved. That you were a good capitalist, a good woman, someone smart and strong and blessed enough to rise to the very top. Your bling was a reflection of your worth. Your bling determined your worth.

Nolita was a diamond among women. A woman whose perfect face, perfect body, perfect smile told everyone that a man who had her had *everything*. For as long as her youth lasted, people would spend money on her like it was water.

Of course, when youth ran out, the consequences hit hard. Hustlers killed each other for money: once markets got saturated, killing someone else's crew was the only way to keep expansion going. Most hustlers were dead or locked up by thirty. Addiction killed their customers by forty.

My mother wasn't a customer, at first. But she ran with the hustlers. Everybody knew how hustlers liked to offer the stuff to the women that they dated. The first hit was always free, and the second and the third and the fourth, if they liked you. By that time your brain was well on its way to being rewired. You woke up from nightmares in a cold sweat if you hadn't had a hit in a couple of days.

Nolita was thirteen when she had me; fourteen by the time she got back out on the streets and started tempting rich men with her looks again. It was what she knew how to do, the only way she knew how to wield power.

It was what kept her safe when she could not rely on her broken mother for love or shelter. It was how she proved her worth to a world that had only ever treated her and her mother as sex objects.

That was why Patty's family sent her, at age 14, to live with extended family she respected. They thought she needed distance from the hood, distance from the places and the people who ran both drugs and Nolita.

Instead, while she was out west, my teenage mother met a 35-year-old man who finally got her started using crack cocaine.

DRUG RUNNER IN DIAPERS

This life that I live, I was given by force,
And these stripes that I wear I ain't given no choice
I was five on the porch, tucking drugs in my jeans
You don't know what I know, never seen what I seen

I was running drugs before I was out of diapers. No joke!

Hustlers knew cops weren't supposed to search young kids. Users knew that every dollar in their pocket was a dollar closer to another high that took them away from the mess of their lives.

I saw their eyes bug out, when they saw money. Saw the way they looked at it like it was life itself. It wasn't greed. It was desperation. They didn't want big-screen TVs or nice cars or anything else you could get with money. They could - and did - sell it all for a hit.

A hit was an escape.

It would go down like this:

The hustlers would pay the users with small kids, real small kids, to put packages in their baby's diapers and carry them across the street, or the town, or wherever the drugs were supposed to go.

By then, my mother was one of those users whose eyes bugged out at the thought of a hit.

I would toddle across crosswalks, bare baby feet over deep cracks in the concrete. Or I'd be carried in my mother's arms across dark streets while she looked sidelong at the world, daring it to challenge her.

You might think she was a bad mother. But in her mind, she didn't have any other options. Doors had been slamming in her face since childhood and after a certain point she'd grown suspicious of anything that looked like an opportunity.

Getting a job, as far as my mother was concerned, was a bad investment. Minimum wage in 1990 was $3.80 per hour, and working meant spending at least forty hours per week focusing on things that didn't interest her for that small pittance.

Around her, hustlers were making tens of thousands per week, paying their people better than the legal jobs would without years of training and tuition. She got paid some of that, for smuggling drugs through cop-heavy areas in my diaper.

Of course, in my mother's case, all that money went to buying drugs.

Most of the people in our neighborhood had the same problems. They could make way more working for a hustler than flipping burgers, and if they or anybody in their family were hooked, they couldn't afford school tuition.

Lots of people *couldn't* get legit work 'cause they had drug convictions on their records - some from all the way back when they were kids.

These were the years of mandatory minimum sentencing, when running crack cocaine was punished like you were working for the devil himself.

Somehow, these were the *same* years when powdered cocaine was so popular with rich white folks that some high-fashion magazines ran straight-up ads for fancy razors and snorting straws.

Some folks got ambitious. It might surprise you to hear that hustlers often *wanted* neighborhood kids to finish school. In these hustler's minds, they were providers, doing what they did so they'd have the power to help lift up their communities. They'd pay neighborhood kids' college tuition when they could, watching with shining eyes the kids who came back with degrees and inevitably moved away.

The hustlers knew folks in their game were not long for this world. That the kids who worked in their crews dropped to ODs, prison sentences, and gang violence like fruit flies with less than 24-hour lives. Hustlers didn't want that for the local kids.

But life happened. Parents and siblings got hooked, got sick, got shot. Legit jobs, where they existed, could be taken away. Parents could be taken away.

And pretty early in life, the ability to fend for yourself was *important* in these hoods. Drugs were where the money was, where the power was, where the glamor was, so it was where ambitious people went to "supply" the need.

People who weren't ambitious went there too, becoming

customers that "demand" their supply. That was my mother.

Instead of schools, I grew up in crack houses.

My mother meant to show she cared, when she took me with her to get high. Meant to say that I was her little man, her best friend, that she would never leave me.

She brought me into the houses with the boarded-up and broken windows - "abandominiums," most of them, buildings nobody cared about. She led or carried me past bodies sprawling on couches or cardboard or mattresses or whatever they could find, sprawling because their minds had taken a total leave of absence from this world. There were old men, young men, old women, young women. Kids. "Adulthood" started around ten years old, in those parts. That was when you were old enough to make serious money, and about a third through your likely life expectancy.

To my mother, there was nothing better than the escape the drugs gave her. She didn't have much to stick around for. Her boyfriend, my father, wanted nothing to do with me, and he was deeper into dope than she was. He sold it and got shot at, and I would see him precious little in my life.

My mother had no friends - not real ones. No job prospects except maybe flipping burgers, if the burger place would hire her without a drug test and a background check first.

She still had men. She still had her body and her smile and men who would give her drugs or shelter, who would tolerate her toddling four-year-old son, in exchange for these things.

In diapers I watched my mother hold the flickering blue flame of a lighter under a spoon until the spoon glowed orange. I watched the rocks melt. I watched her tie off an arm or leg or whatever vein was working that week and shoot up.

I didn't realize that this wasn't normal. That the moans and screams of people on bad trips weren't normal, that the ladies who had sex in corners in exchange for money or a hit were not normal things for a little boy to see.

When my mother was gone, it was like watching someone dream. Her head would roll back and her eyes would close and her whole body relaxed like someone just took all her worries away. It looked so nice, but also scary. It's scary, for a kid, when he can't reach his mom through her drug haze.

When she was awake she was always tense, hunched, haunted, as if she was hunted. Her eyes went wide at the slightest movement, sometimes dark with rage or hatred. She'd look at anybody and anything that moved suddenly like it might be out to get her, out to tell her she was doing something wrong and take her baby away.

But she tried to stay awake as little as possible. Most nights it was me, my mother nodding off, and two or three or four bodies writhing in the corner. To my young mind, this was just what people did.

As I got older I saw ads on TV and billboards. Smiling kids with nice clothes. Smiling families. But they were always white kids, white families. Nothing to tell me that there were kids who looked like me living good lives, too. And even the white families, I thought were fiction. No way anybody smiled that much.

You might wonder where the cops were. Answer: arresting our neighbors. I saw kids and mothers shot and dragged off to jail by cops. I witnessed people who asked them for help turned away with laughter.

Cops were the Big Bad Wolf of my neighborhood. Except, I didn't know the story of the Big Bad Wolf 'cause my mother hadn't picked up a book in ten years. Stories of happy kids with good parents and monsters lurking in the woods held no comfort for her.

To me, this was just all normal.

☆☆☆

Do you know about infantile amnesia? It means baby memories are different from adult memories. The adult brain can't read the baby memories - so most of us can't remember damn near anything that happened to us before we were three.

Those years are *important*. They teach our bodies, at a deep level, what to expect about the world. Maybe those first few years were why I was so faithful to my mother: my body remembered how she took care of me before.

But *I* didn't remember it. As far as I knew, we'd always lived in abandominiums, taken weekends off in crack houses. As far as I knew, there wasn't anything else in the whole world.

I saw smiling families on billboard ads and I knew, in some part of my mind, that there were well-dressed folks walking the streets in other parts of town. But to me as a kid, these people were like fairy tales. They did not belong to the same world as myself. It didn't help that almost all of them were white, and I was not.

My Aunt Patty was an exception. She was like some magical creature who would bring us food and clothes every so often. She spoke to my mother so kindly, so gently, like I never saw anyone do.

Around Aunt Patty, my mother became like a child. She took up the same mannerisms, the little shyness, as a child who is guilty but also pleased to have an adults' attention. Those were the only times she didn't stand tall, her head up and her eyes watchful, like she was in charge but also afraid.

Among the things I didn't know was that my mother *was* a child. She turned eighteen the same year I turned four.

That was around the time she met the bravest man I have ever known.

CHARLES

Gotta thank Uncle Phil
He brought me in, changed my life
He showed me how family feel
And how to recognize what's real
U even changed my heart
And half the ways that I feel
But it's time for me to wake up
'Cause I keep dreaming I'm Will

Charles met my mother in a courtyard, off a long stretch of cracked West Baltimore sidewalk. He was chillin', enjoying the neighborhood like people did before smartphones and computers became the center of attention. Back then, there was only the neighborhood to enjoy - your neighbors, your people, and whatever craziness they were getting up to.

My mother, only a few years into the depths of her addiction, was still one of the most beautiful women you would ever meet. She will forever live in my mind that way - as a woman who was beautiful, whose beauty was *important* to her, whose curves turned the head of any man who saw her and whose smile was like daybreak and Vogue magazine all rolled into one.

Charles met her in a courtyard outside an apartment complex. He saw her smile, he saw the desperation hiding beneath her goodness. He got hooked on protecting her.

My mother sensed something in Charles that she had not sensed in many other men. He was not the wealthiest man on the block; certainly not the 'baddest,' by standards of the day. He *was* big and strong and kind to her. He was also one of the few people in our neighborhood that worked a legit job long-term, which meant he made far less than the hustlers, but also created a life for himself with a vision untainted by the devastation surrounding us.

Charles was clean. In our hood, that required tremendous force of will. It required tremendous dedication to something - an ideal , a vision- that he found more important than the twin siren songs of radical escape and radical wealth.

My mother, with one baby on her hip and a second on the way, was beginning to recognize strength of character when she saw it. Nolita saw the strength she needed in Charles.

Charles recognized Nolita. He saw the dazzling woman and the lost child both. He saw the woman who could love, on her good days, fiercely. He saw the mother, and the daughter, in need of protection.

He saw me at her side, lost and in need of guidance. He saw the child of a mother who didn't know what 'home' meant herself.

Within a year, we were all living together. Patty's family had helped my mother and Charles to secure a real house, with utilities and everything, and Charles' job was enough to pay the bills. He poured his heart and soul into our family.

For me, the biggest change was the comfort and security.

Suddenly, we had a refrigerator, food, running water, electricity. In the abandominiums, this made you rich! More than that: my mother had jewelry, and I had video game systems. Charles was determined that this family would have the best of everything.

He called my mother his wife. His commitment to her was absolute. They didn't marry on the books, that would have ended my mother's eligibility for the program that allowed her and me and my brand new little sister to see doctors.

Lots of people didn't get married because they didn't want to lose benefits in my neighborhood. The politicians who wanted to cut public spending had done more harm than good. When a family with five kids could lose access to state-provided healthcare long before they could afford to buy it on their own, making too much money or getting legally married started to look downright irresponsible.

But in Charles' heart, they were married.

Life with Charles was the best I could remember. Some things he did that I didn't like - disciplining me, telling me that there was a right and a wrong way - I now recognize as a great gift. Charles wanted me to have the same strength of character he had, when I grew up.

If he could, Charles would have been at home with the family. He loved being a husband and dad more than anything. But keeping his job as a construction supervisor meant spending almost all his waking hours away from home. That was how he provided for us without ever resorting to the drug trade.

Charles hated drugs.

He especially hated them where my mother was concerned.

The bravest thing I've ever seen was Charle's love for her. He'd tell hustlers not to sell to Nolita. Tell them like he meant business.

These were men who were known for violence - for shooting anybody who might put a damper on their hustle. Here was this man I called my dad, this family man, approaching them on the basketball courts where they played. On the street corners where they supervised. Telling them they'd better stay away from his wife.

This happened not once, but many times.

I remember watching on one time, watching him with my fingers twisted in the little squares of a chain link fence while the dribbling of a basketball slowed and stopped like a heartbeat. I could feel the tension in my bones as they stopped to look at him.

I could see that at least two of the dudes were packing. I'd learned, by that age, to recognize an armed man by the way he walks, by the way his hands hover near his pants, or maybe his ankle. I would have been about six years old.

I couldn't hear the words, but I could see the gestures. The posturing. The hustlers fronting, threatening - and then nodding. Understanding.

It might surprise you that almost all the dudes Charles asked agreed to stay away from my mother. Business is a hustler's life, but all of them are sons, brothers, fathers, too. So when a man who is known for doing the right thing asks you to stay away from his wife, you do it.

It eventually got to the point that no local hustlers would sell to Nolita. Charles tried with all his might to help her quit. He gave her everything she needed. A comfortable home. All the love a person could ever imagine. The kind of love that makes you risk your life, not once, but many times. The kind of love where nothing matters more than the person you love.

But that didn't stop Nolita from using.

Sometimes she would have her friends pick up drugs for her, from other parts of town. They'd smuggle them over and Nolita would pay them - selling her jewelry, my game systems, the food in the refrigerator to pay for it.

Sometimes she would go to crack houses across town, be gone for days at a time. Sometimes she would take me with her.

Always, Charles would go get her if he came home to find her gone.

I spent a lot of time on both sides of the crack house doors.

With Nolita, inside, hiding. She still took me with her sometimes - I was still her little man, her security blanket. She trained me and all the other junkies to hide when Charles came knocking, to pretend the house was empty.

It never worked. He'd stand out there banging on the door and hollering until he got his Nolita. Until the hustlers forced her out 'cause they were afraid the cops would come if he kept standing there yelling.

Other times I'd be outside with him. He would come home to find her gone, to find me there, and he knew that she'd be quicker to come out for me than just for him. He also knew that there was nothing that I hadn't seen.

So he would take me by the hand. "Hawk," he would say, "we're going to get your mother."

Then he'd stand outside the crack house door with or without me, banging and hollering for his Nolita, until somebody made her come out. They'd hustle her outside, then, throw her into the arms of her husband. He'd drive all three of us home, begging and pleading with her to stop the habit that he knew would someday kill her.

In the end, Nolita became Charles' drug. One that would have proved deadly if he didn't walk away from his addiction to her.

Nolita saw this, and I think the bravest thing she ever did was breaking up with him. It was not that she didn't like him, or did not love him anymore. It was that she loved him too much.

The addict in her must have loved his money more than she could say. Without Charles' income, she'd be back to getting hits only when she could scrape together $10, or $20, or $50 without a steady job. She would have no stability. She would be miserable.

But if she stayed with Charles, someday he would die. He would challenge the wrong hustler, knock on the wrong crack house door.

The man had lived his whole life clean, had done everything to become a provider instead of a pusher. But he'd still end up on the wrong end of some fiend's or hustler's bullet if my mother let him stay around.

So that was why my mother left Charles: because she didn't want to get him killed.

Because she loved him more than she loved crack.

THE CHAMPION

In this world you can't cry if ur a man, why?
Cause there's rules on how to be a man, right?
So we supposed to be strong no matter what,
Suck it up, cause if u cry ur a chump
(That's what the world say)
Then they wonder why we like this,
Cause in our chest it's a heart filled with ice chips
Pumping cold blood straight thru our veins
Then them thoughts in our brain
Will drive a brother insane
(Man this world shady)

Something happened when I was a kid that my stepdad never knew about.

People will do crazy things when their brains start screaming at them for crack. That is the drug's power. After a while, it doesn't feel good anymore. But the cravings don't have anything to do with wanting to feel good. They're about wanting the craving to stop. The drug hijacks the brain's dopamine system, its motivation circuit that tells us what we have to do to stay alive.

To an addict, crack withdrawal feels like drowning.

Fiends do all kinds of crazy things to stay in dope. By the time I was six, my mother knew all of them. She knew about the sex trade. She knew how to mug people. And she knew about the fight clubs.

Blood sports have always had a crowd. You probably know about Michael Vick's dogfighting rings, or the cockfighting rings where people tie razor blades to rooster's ankles and make them go at each other. You might even have heard about the fiends who'll fight *each other* for money, taking hits for audience's entertainment in exchange for a few bucks.

What you probably don't know about is the fighting rings for *children.*

Anything that can fight, people have fought it. In Baltimore there were people who fought children, figuring 'kids fight anyway.' But this wasn't ahli good-sport boxing match or boys-being-boys kind of situation.

This was parents standing around, hollering at kids that they'd better not lose or they're getting beat even worse when they get home. This was mom's pride, mom's happiness, mom's safety on the line. 'Cause if the kid lost, then their mom or dad or aunt or uncle wouldn't have money for crack, you see? Sometimes, they wouldn't have money for food either.

I had a unique advantage. I was taught by master boxers.

I was introduced to them at Mack Lewis gym. I don't know if my mother arranged it because she already had the idea to fight me in her head, or if that came later. But either way, I fell hard for the star power of the instructors there - some of them were household names among boxing fans. And Charles was happy to pay for anything that made me happy - especially something, he thought, that would teach me discipline and self-improvement.

I was good. I was *especially* good because I knew my mother needed me to be a fighter. I believed my mother needed my protection. She'd spent all the years I could remember in distress, needing someone to feed her, take care of her, comfort her.

When I was good enough, she took me to this back alley fighting ring and set me up against another kid from the neighborhood. One look into my mother's eyes and I felt unbeatable.

These matches could be held almost anywhere. In somebody's backyard - then at least the ground was dirt-soft when you landed on it. More often, though, they were in basements or back alleys, with other kids keeping lookout, running to tell the adults so they could put on a good front if any cops came by.

Before each match, my mother would look down at me from her height that seemed, to a six-year-old, impossibly tall. She would stare down her nose at me judgmentally, disdainfully, and say: "You better win."

I never lost.

The first time, I didn't know what was happening. I'd seen kids get into fights, but never 'cause adults told them to. I'd fought with the best, sparred with them, but they never hit me *hard*.

This was bareknuckle, adrenaline-fueled, and I think me and the other kid were both scared and confused. He'd done this before, I gathered, but he wasn't very good at it. He tended to get his ass beat, but his family kept fighting him in hopes he'd start winning them money. My mother had wanted to start me against someone easy.

He started punching, *really* punching, not graceful and not strong - his fists had the weakness of fear behind them - but hard enough.

As his fists pummeled my jaw, my cheekbone, my head, something in me snapped.

I started throwing punches just like the big names had taught me, dodging and weaving like we practiced. When someone knows how to carry their weight, how to be ready to shift to avoid or respond to a hit, it's almost impossible to knock them down. When someone knows how to throw their whole body behind their fist, punching not just with their arms but with their everything, they can hit *hard.*

The other kid was out cold in about thirty seconds. The adults were cheering, surprised, amazed, delighted. People were practically throwing money at my mother, and she was smiling wider than I'd seen in a while.

That started my rise to my first, worst kind of fame. For a couple of years, I was the neighborhood champion.

I never lost a match. Ever. My training and the paralyzing fear of disappointing my mother made an explosive combination. I wasn't the biggest kid, or the fastest, but I was the sure thing.

Everybody who knew about the fights recognized me. I became a neighborhood celebrity. Our neighborhood didn't have a lot of things going for it, a lot of things that it was best at. But child fighting - now it had that.

I was their sure thing to bet on when they needed cash. I was their Christmas bonus and their local sports team all wrapped into one. I think a lot of them thought I actually enjoyed the fights, the status, the success. Like I was a pro athlete living the dream or something.

I hated it, of course. I hated beating up other kids like me with every fiber of my being. But you don't say that when your ma's looking at you with those eyes that say you'll catch hell at home if you say it out loud. You don't say it when your ma doesn't *want* you to, when you're certain it would hurt her somehow.

Charles never knew. He worked about twelve hours a day to support us. Plus, I always won so I didn't get beat up as badly as the other kids. What bruises I did come home with could easily be explained as "boys being boys," or souvenirs from my boxing classes.

You know how boxers and athletes develop "routines" that they do before games to get in the zone? Here was mine:

My mother would walk me back to wherever the match was happening. There would be kids from different neighborhoods - it was almost like a regional championship. But they didn't standardize weight classes very well. Some kids were older than me, some younger, some skinny, some round. It was whoever's family was desperate or greedy enough to try to make a buck off of their kids' blood. I was often one of the smallest, but I was fierce, and I was skilled.

We'd step into the room and my mother would look down at me with that look that made me desperate. That look that said that all her hopes were riding on me - and all her anger, too.

"You'd better win," she would say. She didn't need to tell me what would happen if I didn't.

My mother would glare down at me and I would nod dutifully, and she knew that meant I was gonna win. I would fight the devil if that meant I could give her heaven and she saw it in my eyes. She would study my face, then go place bets.

Before the fight began, I would find a corner and cry.

Truthfully, I never liked hurting anybody. Not even when adults told me it was a good thing to do. I had eyes- I could see that the other kids were gonna catch hell when they got home. I could see that they too were only doing it because somebody made them. Once in a blue moon you ran across a kid who did *like* the game, a big guy whose size and fists were the only power he'd had in all his life. But their love of the sport never lasted long after they fought me. I laid 'em all down, for my mother.

So I would cry and cry and cry in my corner for a few minutes before the match started. Then I'd be ready. I'd analyze the other kids' movements, pinpoint their weak spots and imbalances, almost mechanically. I'd take them out, end it, as efficiently as I could. I couldn't wait for it to be over.

My boxing teachers taught me a lot. They taught me how to power through pain and stay focused. They taught me how to keep fighting with blood in your eyes, because sometimes that happened in professional boxing. They taught me how to hold your fist right so that when you hit another kid, it was his teeth that broke and not your fingerbones.

They assumed I'd be doing it all with gloves on, of course, and with rules. I don't like to think about what they might have done if they'd walked in on one of these basement matches.

This is how it happened:

Picture a backyard filled with the highest and lowest players on the hood's totem pole. There is a high wooden fence around the yard and houses who had an understanding with the owner on either side, so anyone can do anything they want out in the open.

The drug hustlers are there in lawn chairs, with their sharp clothes and gorgeous women. These are the ones who have a taste for bloody action, for feeling superior to somebody else.

The fiends and the homeless people who need cash are there, keeping a respectful distance from the hustlers so their scent doesn't waft upwind.

The sex workers are there - from high-end glamour to sick, skinny fiends, for anybody who might be buying after the bets are paid out.

I am there too. Me and some other terrified children.

On this day, I fight a kid who's smaller than me. This isn't all that common. I'm one of the smaller ones on the circuit, one of the younger ones. This kid is probably my age, but looks like he might have gotten fed even less as a baby. He's scared.

And because he's scared, I get the drop on him easily. In twenty seconds I've got him laid out, straddling him, landing punches to his face. I am focused on his face, so I can see clearly when he turns his head, when his eyes seek his mother in the crowd with a pleading expression. I hesitate.

I could not hear what the kid's mother said to him, over the chanting and hollering over the crowd, over the 'finish him' coming from my mom and one of the big hustlers. But her lips move, and this kid's expression changes. Something black comes over him. His face contorts, becomes demonic.

He turns on me and *charges.*

I don't know where a kid that little got a strength that big. In a minute I'm flying back - that's nothing new. But then comes explosion of stars, and the darkness in one side of my vision.

It takes a minute for it to start to hurt. It's the corner of the back porch steps. I've nailed my head on the sharp edge of a wooden board, and the world is dim and ringing. Nothing feels real.

The other kid is coming down on me, wailing on me, punch after punch, just like I was doing to him. Instinctively, my eyes seek my mother where she stands, half crouching, fists balled and pumping like she's watching a sporting match.

Her words are dim - I almost can hear them - but I guess every kid's got special ears for his mother's voice.

"Shake him off," her screams come to me faintly, through the ringing and the haze. "Get up and shake him off! I ain't raise no crybaby!"

As she says *crybaby,* her face twisted in dissatisfaction, and I push him back.

I don't know how. To this day I don't know how. I only know that the other kid is suddenly on the ground, I've got blood in my eyes, but my teachers taught me to fight around that.

They did *not* teach me to choke somebody out, but you do what you've got to do when your ma is in danger, in danger of not getting paid, in danger of being disappointed.

My hands are around this other kids' throat - an easy tactic, a merciful one. He's out cold in less than sixty seconds. No more bruises or concussions or broken bones. Just sleep. I don't know what will happen to him when he gets home, but I know I did my ma proud.

These adults, the ones who organize the matches, always step in and stop them when somebody passes out. Like they need to. Like the kids are ever gonna keep going, keep fighting when nobody's telling them they have to.

This time the officiator, a big guy who feels entirely too proud of his role here, takes my little bloodied fist in his hand and raises my arm high.

"The champion!" he declares, like he was announcing a game at Memorial Stadium.

He parades me around for a minute while all the adults clap and cheer and the world starts to ring a little less. The hustlers are clapping their hands together slow, big grins on their faces like they've just seem something great, something that's gonna live in history. Their ladies are smiling and applauding politely, not caring about nothing except agreeing with their men. The prostitutes and homeless dudes are already swarming the guy with the cash, whose job it is to dispense the winnings.

I was grinning when I left with my mother, her little wad of cash winnings tucked in her bra between her twenty-something breasts.

That grin didn't last long.

As soon as we hit the street, out of sight of the others, my mother grabbed the front of my shirt. Her facade of victory was gone; she looked furious.

"You don't *ever* let them see you hurt," she hissed, picking me up by my shirt. "You don't *ever* let them think they have a shot at beating you." I recognized the rage in her face, then: it was the same rage the other kid had had, right before he charged me. There was something terrible and haunted behind it.

"You're *my* son. And we don't ever let them see us hurt. *Understand?*"

And then I was apologizing. The pain in my head, the blood in my eyes, the brief rush of victory all forgotten in the face of my mother's cold rage.

"I'm sorry, ma. I'm sorry, I'm sorry - "

Back in the day, I didn't think much of anything. As a young kid, you think, you *feel* what adults want you to think and feel. How your ma says it is is how it *is*. What your ma says is right is right, what she says is important is important. You forget about anything else.

I forgot everything except that I had almost shamed my mother. I had almost made us look weak. And that could *not* happen, ever again. That was just how it was. That was what was important.

Now I look back on her eyes that day. I think I see some haunted fear underneath that rage, I think maybe she was talking to herself as much as to me when she gave that lecture.

And I wonder who it was that taught Nolita to never, ever look weak.

OLD ENOUGH

Where I'm from u don't make it out
And the young niggaz u don't see them smile
Their mother high they their father gone
They tryna keep warm in a vacant house
They gotta put food in their siblings' mouths
The number one he don't know how
He a young boy and gotta figure it out now

When I was about ten years old, the local hustlers decided I was old enough to work on their crew.

Having kids work for the crew was common. Kids were sharp-eyed and quick on their feet, grateful for money, and not a lot of us were going to school anyway.

I'd been helping out with the business, to some extent, ever since my mother became a customer. Vials were smuggled in my diapers, where no cop would ever dare to look.

But at ten, I'd shown responsibility. I was a caretaker for my brothers and sisters. I'd shown fearless determination as a champion fighter. And most of all, the hustlers knew my mother. And they knew I'd do anything for her.

They started kids off small. First, I was playing look-out. Kids could sit on benches or stoops, or ride up and down the streets on their bikes - normal kid things to do. But these kids were chosen, sometimes, for their ability to run fast. And they were trained in certain cues - a whistle, or sometimes a codeword - that let any hustler in the vicinity know that cops were nearby.

Then, it was a small-time hustle. There were lots of standardized different types of vials containing different amounts of crack. They sold for $5, $10, $20, $50. The hustlers would give a kid ten or twenty of the smaller vials, tell them to sell them and bring the money back. If the kid unloaded the vials in a reasonable amount of time and brought back the right amount of money, they'd get more.

You sold 'em like this: on street corners, in front of convenience stores, you could tell a fiend a mile away. Most of 'em who had been using for more than a few months walked a certain way, had a certain look in their eyes. Even if they weren't all broken down from the addiction, even if they were one of those rich white folks coming into the hood to get their product, they'd look around like birds of prey as they walked, scanning for some little hustler with vials.

When one of them got close enough, you'd chant or sing. Something like:

"Ten-dollar-twenty-dollar-fifty-dollar." All the types of vials you had. "Red-top-blue-top-grey-top." Like a commercial jingle, it became so automatic to your brain you didn't even think about it. You were your own little walking billboard that only came on when a likely customer was near.

The vials went real fast. Crack has regulars like no other

industry. You sell somebody a small vial, all likelihood is they'll be back within a few hours looking for another one. You sell 'em a big vial, you can bet they'll be back within a few days, probably with friends.

The distributors split the payment for the vials about 80-20 with the kids who hustled for them. That meant a kid who sold ten of the $10 vials - an easy day's work - got $20. Once you started getting trusted with large amounts of larger vials, you could bring in hundreds of dollars a week easy.

That was *damn* good money for hood kids, or for hood adults for that matter.

I'd always been a big brother, taking care of my brothers and sisters when they were too young to take care of themselves. I'd always been the one who made things work around the house, when for most of my life no adults were doing that.

Turned out, that made me a natural leader.

When I started hustling, it was just natural for me to go around to other kids on the nearby blocks to see how their hustling was going. I made sure no one was messing with 'em, no one was stiffing 'em, made sure they were getting the right amount of money to turn in to the distributors. If they were having trouble, I suggested how they could improve the routes, or their tactics. Sometimes I'd shuffle things up, suggesting that two kids swap routes if I thought it would suit them better.

Within a couple of months, I was basically an unofficial block manager - all the kids would come to me with their problems and their money, I'd count out the money to make sure they had the right amount and advise them how to solve their problems.

It didn't take long for the OGs to notice.

In the hood, "OG" stands for "Original Gangster." These are dudes who have been around for a while and have achieved great success. They lived in the same neighborhood, the same community as you, but they had money, power, and respect. They had all the status symbols - sports cars, motorcycles, big gold chains, rings, slick hats, slick outfits.

Those were just the outward signs of their true power - they had the kind of money that let them pay other people's mortgages and college tuition, let them help build churches and send local kids on field trips that were some of the best days of our lives.

They were providers. They were proficient businessmen. They were our models of success. In the hood, we didn't live next-door to any black doctors or lawyers or business owners. People who made success the legal way moved away as soon as they had the bucks to do so.

But the OGs stayed. And so they were the *only* role models, the only models of black success we saw in our everyday lives. Black doctors and lawyers were kind of fairy tale creatures, things that existed on TV but not in real life.

Of course, all the OGs got their money from hustling. They were the guys who made big deals, bought whole bricks of powdered coke from guys who had 'em flown in from Colombia or wherever, turned that raw material into crack rocks that delivered eleven minutes of high per hit to residents of the hood.

The OGs got to where they were - that rich, and still alive - by being smart. A smart OG knew a good thing when he saw it, and a little kid who can run a block, solve problems, who goes around making sure everything's working well for everyone even though nobody told him to, is a good thing.

My OG was an old guy, to still be in the game - probably thirty-something and all in one piece, dripping bling and fly fashion, driving the kind of sports car I'd drool over in magazines.

"Yo, Shorty," the OG said, rolling up in his pearl-white corvette, "I talk to you for a minute?"

I ran over dutifully and stood respectfully silent.

"I see you doing good work out here, Shorty. Taking care of all my other little hustlers. You doing real good. From now on, Imma make it official. You're my deputy, Shorty. You report to me, and I'll tell all these other little hustlers to do what you tell 'em to."

I swelled with pride. Not about getting to tell other kids what to do - I was already doing that. But I'd been recognized for doing something good. That was a rare thing.

And this was the most important industry to be good at.

I may have been ten, but I wasn't stupid. I'd had to strategize, from a very young age, about how to get the most out of what I had. So instead of buying expensive clothes or jewelry or game systems, I saved the money I made on my ever-expanding hustle.

I saved a *lot*. By the time I was eleven, I'd saved enough to buy an eighth of a brick of powdered coke.

I *knew* that was how much money I had, because I paid attention when the OGs talked. I knew what the raw materials were worth. But you couldn't just *buy* an eighth like walking down to the corner store.

Buying powder in bulk meant you were about to start

competing in a big way. If you were cooking your own rocks, managing your own small army of distributors, it meant you were a proper businessman. For that, you needed permission. You had to get a blessing from your OG.

Mine was happy to give it.

First off, I'd be buying from him - which meant he could buy more raw materials and get it cooked, distributed, and paid for.

Second, there is this weird mentorship thing among hustlers. Competition is dangerous, but the sense of community is strong. You want young guys in your hood to grow up to be something great.

For some OGs, that means *forbidding* certain kids from hustling and making 'em read books and go to school instead. For others, it means mentoring them on how to be the best hustlers they can be.

Young, up-and-coming hustlers are good. As long as they're from your hood, and not a neighboring hood that's trying to take over your customers.

Long story short, my OG approved. I gave him my savings, he gave me an eighth of a brick. I called my crew of other ten-year-olds, and we started cooking.

Cooking crack is one of the basic skills that anyone who's been hustling for any length of time learns. All you're doing, really, is making all the little granules of powdered cocaine stick together. In the process, you make it so it vaporizes really easy, and can be smoked.

You do this by cooking powdered coke with water and

baking soda - and sometimes a little extra. People trying to stretch their raw materials might add other drugs, or I even heard of one case of some crazy kid adding vitamins, trying to make more rocks for less money.

That's why there's competition among different 'brands' of crack. Everybody knows that different distributors cook differently, be it through incompetence or artistry or attempts at cutting corners. What one distributor does or does not add decides what the quality of the high is. A low-quality rock might be cheaper to produce, but it only gets desperate customers who are likely to defect as soon as they get enough money to afford the good stuff.

My crew cooked good stuff - and I had brand appeal for another reason. Once, I'd been The Champion. The fighter kid nobody ever beat. Even though I was just eleven years old, people had respect for me. Manly respect. And being the local equivalent of a sports star, it turned out, had its marketing advantages. Me endorsing crack was like Michael Jordan endorsing Nikes.

Then, things got even crazier. When my OG got locked up, everybody agreed that there was nobody better-suited to take over his operation than me. I knew even bigger connects - the rich white dudes who sold bricks to the OGs through my mother, who'd been in the game for most of her life. I knew the routes and the tricks. Most importantly, I knew the people.

If I'd stayed where I was, hustling for money and getting it, my life might have been very different. I had no real concept of a life beyond the one I knew. I knew that people died from the game all the time - of overdoses, of gunshot wounds. But nobody knew any different way to do it. There were no black lawyers or doctors in the hood, no good schools or universities. Those were faraway things - not for us.

If I'd stayed where I was, I might've become an OG – might have had status for a moment or two,, until I got locked me up or someone put a bullet through me sometime in my twenties.

Lucky for me, fate had other plans.

PATTY'S CHILDREN

So I look north to the star,
Tryna crawl my way out of the cave
Without leaving a scar
But it's hard when u raised like this
Even harder when ur mind caged like this

While I succeeded in my hustle, at home, everything went to hell.

By the time Nolita kicked Charles out, I was the only one of Nolita's kids who was old enough to remember living without electricity or running water. Those things went away again real quick without Charles' steady paycheck and general sense of responsibility.

My mother kept the house, which her family had helped pay for. But all the good things stopped coming. Soon, it was candlelight and whatever food we could scrounge up out in the neighborhood with what my mother didn't spend on crack.

She didn't get enough crack without Charles' money buying things that she could pawn, so she was a mess. I'd find her often sprawling on the couch, or curled up in a corner by candlelight, just out of it, trying to forget about the world.

Five years with Charles had given her five kids. As the oldest person in the house who wasn't a cracked-out mess, taking care of my younger siblings fell to me.

I learned how to do that pretty fast. Small amounts of money could be gotten by helping local hustlers with minor tasks, by sweeping the floors of local barber shops, by begging. Eventually, I had hustling money - good money. But that took a little while.

For a few months, it was just the six of us: me, my brothers and sisters, and my mother, in that darkened and rapidly deteriorating house. I don't quite know how the rats got in, but soon they were chewing at the floorboards, chewed holes in the carpet at some places, and I'd have to chase them out of my little brothers' and sisters' rooms.

My mother, she just tried not to go crazy.

Foster care came for the younger kids a few months out. It was probably because my siblings had knocked on the neighbors' door in the wee hours of the morning, asking for food. Folks in our neighborhood were pretty understanding of families in hard times, but eventually it became clear that things weren't gonna get better. Cop cars showed up in the driveway, bringing a small army of officers and social workers.

I ran. That was what my mother had trained me to do, what the hustlers I worked for reinforced. Any time you see cops, run. They don't mean nothing good for you. So I slipped out the back door and vanished, jogging along through neighbors' backyards, weaving a path across sidewalks that no sane adult would be able to follow. I knew my first priority, same as my mother's: don't get caught.

When I came back hours later, late, late into the night, my siblings were gone. Only my mother was left, alone with a candle in the corner of the living room, crying. I went to her and curled up in her arms.

I later learned that Charles got all his kids. As their biological dad, he had as much right to them as Nolita. And he was clearly the more fit parent.

Much, *much* later, I found out Charles tried to get me too. He'd argued, begged, pleaded with the courts, said he effectively my common-law dad after being with my mom for five years. But my genes weren't his and there were no legal documents showing him as family. As far as the system was concerned he and I had no relationship.

When getting parental rights failed, he tried to qualify as a foster parent to take me in. But he couldn't meet the requirements. With a single income and my mother keeping the house, he couldn't afford enough bedrooms to raise his kids *and* qualify to foster an "unrelated" child. He turned his brain inside out trying to find a way to keep me safe and with family. But the way the state saw it, he wasn't my family.

Oh well. I would've run away from him, like I did from the first twelve foster families who took me on.

I avoided the cops and social workers for months. When I saw a strange car coming, or came home to see one in the driveway, I bolted. If there was one thing that ten years with Nolita had taught me, it was how to fend for myself. I could go anywhere, stay anywhere, get anything I needed on my own and there wasn't a damn thing the state could do about it.

When foster care finally got me, it was only because my

mother helped them do it.

They'd dropped off the social workers and the cops, I guess, and then driven the cars around the block so I wouldn't see them outside the house. They'd sat my mother down at the kitchen table, opened the blinds to let light in so it was almost like the electricity had come back on, and talked to her.

When I got home, everything on the outside of the house looked normal. But I opened the door and immediately knew something was wrong. My mother *never* opened the kitchen blinds. She preferred to live in darkness, hiding the wreck that was the inside of the house from the world.

I saw her sitting in a chair at the table, waiting for me. That was also wrong. My mother never sat like that, in a chair, her back straight and her hands folded all proper in her lap. She looked ashamed.

I walked toward her, trembling.

"Hawk," my mother said softly, in her sweet little child voice. "I need you to go with these people." Only then, as I walked into the kitchen, could I see the others. A lady in a blazer, a man in a dress shirt, two uniformed officers. All watched me apprehensively, waiting for me to run.

"Hawk, you know I love you, and all your brothers and sisters."

I nodded. I'm not sure if I believed it, but I knew she wanted me to.

"Well the thing is - I can't have your brothers and sisters back unless I get my act together. And I don't think I can take care of you, dear, while I do that. So I need you to go with them for a while, Hawk. You know I love you."

I stood there, shaking. Looking from my mother to the others. I could tell she didn't *really* want to do this, but I could also tell she *sort of* did.

What was my mother going to do without me?

"I really need you to go with them, Hawk. I'll see you again. I just - need to take some time for me, right now."

I knew that 'me time,' for my mother just meant time curled up in the corner with a candle, crying, not eating, but I said nothing. She was my ma. However she said it was was how it was.

The lady in the blazer stepped out of the corner, hesitantly.

"Hawk," she asked, "are you gonna run away?"

I looked at my mother. She shook her head. I shook mine.

"Good," the lady looked visibly relieved. She crept toward me, almost the way you might creep up on a stray cat you don't want to scare, and, hesitantly, reached for my hand.

My mother nodded. I took the lady's hand.

The lady led me out to her car, clutching my hand like it was a dog's leash, like she might use it to stop me if I bolted.

"I'm so glad you see that we're trying to help you, Hawk," she said with forced cheerfulness. "Now, we're going to go see your new home!"

My stomach flipped, all butterflies, and not the good kind, when she said that.

It turned out my instinct was right.

✩✩✩

In the first home, the foster parents burned kids as punishment. There was a science to it. Heat a spoon over the gas flame of the stove, flick it on the skin. It'd hurt like hell without leaving marks for the social workers to find.

I climbed out a window at night, took a bike some kid had left laying in his front yard, biked back to my mother's house, and curled up with her where she was sleeping on the living room floor.

The social workers came for me again the next day. Again, Nolita asked me to go with them.

After a while, this became normal. We had a drill.

I'd get placed with a new foster family. If they were cruel to me, I'd bolt; if they were kind to me, I'd stick it out until the thought of my mother alone in that house became too much to bear. I think my record was six weeks.

When I bolted, I'd go back to my mother's house - on foot, by stolen bike, by bus ticket bought with change I'd scrounged up in any imaginable way. I found my way to my mother from anywhere in the greater Baltimore area, like she was a homing beacon or something.

The social workers would come collect me the next day, and I would go with them because my mother said so. Though she never seemed upset when I came home again. More like relieved.

After a while my social worker wouldn't even be pissed. It'd be one of those 'another day, another dollar' situations where I got back into her car real quietly and neither of us even said anything.

But after about the twelfth time, she locked the car doors and turned to me, real serious.

"Hawk," she said, "you have to stop doing this."

I squirmed. What did she expect me to say? What did she expect me to do?

"If you don't," she said, "they're going to put you in lockup. One of those detention centers with the highest level of security they're allowed to give minors. You wouldn't like one of those places at all. I don't what that for you. So how can we make this work?"

I thought about it. I wouldn't normally have bothered to think about it, but I was getting tired of running. Getting tired of coming home to see my mother, always as desperate as before, never improved. I was pretty sure she was never going to get any of her kids back - not legally, anyway. I was pretty sure she was never going to make the system happy, and she wasn't making me real happy right now anyway.

There had to be something better.

I hesitated for a long, guilty moment before I said: "Patty. My Aunt Patty."

My social workers' ears perked up at that.

"My Aunt Patty - my ma knows her number. She used to come check on us when I was younger. Bring us food and stuff."

What I really remembered most about Patty was that she had always been kind and gentle with my mother, like no adult I had ever seen except for Charles. That had to make her good people. Maybe she would let me see my mother if I stayed with her. They were family, right?

My social worker made a phone call.

☆☆☆

My Aunt Patty was crazy rich. Not by TV-family standards, but by every standard I had ever known to be real.

She had a house. A *nice* house in a *nice* neighborhood, where cops stopped crime instead of stealing and greeted you with a nod instead of a glare. There were bushes and flower beds in the front. I tried to imagine someone having enough time on their hands to take care of a flower bed.

My Aunt was happy to see me, but also sad. I understand that now. Always happy to see me. Sad that her niece had lost the house, lost Charles. Sad, like I was, that Nolita had no one to take care of her. That she couldn't keep anyone around her.

But she stood tall and smiled cool and professional as she spoke to the social worker. She was kind like the oblivious foster parents, but dignified like the people I grew up with. Dignified like someone who knows that her existence might depend on having everything in order. That she can't afford to cut corners. It was a lesson we'd both learned, and it made me feel better to see that she understood.

If I trusted anybody, I trusted her.

I looked around her house in amazement. The carpet was so fresh and clean and soft, I wanted to bury my face in it. The furniture was like it was right off one of the commercials on TV. Her home had a warm, sweet smell to it - until that point, I'm not sure I ever smelled *clean* except for the antiseptic kind of clean that hospitals and furniture stores had.

There were toys, books, pictures, everywhere. I tried to imagine anybody looking at this wealth and not trying to sell it for cash or drugs.

"Hawk," my Aunt Patty said, "this is your room. It's also my son Michael's room. You two will be sharing, so you've got to take care of each other. Okay?"

The room was small compared to the living room and dining room, but that somehow just made it cool. Like a secret hideout. Light leaked through the thick curtains covering the windows, and the room had shelves that were covered in toy robots, cars, and dinosaurs. There were bunk beds - one bed stacked on top of another. I imagined Michael and I whispering to each other, conspiring at night like on sleepovers on TV.

"Hawk," Aunt Patty said, "welcome home."

I got to know Aunt Patty's children.

Michael was five or six, and he was my best friend in this family. He was the same age as my siblings, the ones with Charles. Michael was sweet and cheerful and loved to ride bikes and play in the creek out back. I played with him and watched him like a hawk, flaring up all protective when anybody came near. My body hadn't learned what safety was yet, and as when I was around, God help anyone who fucked with Michael.

There was Karlie. A couple years younger than me and sassy as hell, but she followed my aunt's rules or faced consequences. I was beginning to get the concept, living here, that consequences can be good. Little consequences, that stop you from hitting life-destroying consequences later. Karlie was also some kind of genius, or something. She was actually ahead of me in school, some special school for kids who are too smart for normal school.

Sheila was in high school. She was nice to me, but I barely saw her. As a teenager, the last thing she wanted was to get saddled with child drama - or worse, babysitting duty. She was a good young woman. But she was only human, and just figuring out what being a woman is all about.

The last of my aunt's kids, Phillip, was in college. I'd never admit it, but inside I pretty much worshipped him. He was studying something or another that's going to let him be successful - have a career, and a house like this one. I mostly just knew that he was into video games and wrestling, like me, that he'd talk to me and treat me just like a kid brother when he came home. We both thought sports cars were about the coolest thing in the world, and he already had a bright red camaro. He said it was a gift from Aunt Patty.

I tried to imagine anyone's mom being able to give them something like that. And without even hustling.

Living at Aunt Patty's meant I had to go to school. That was pretty new to me.

I'd been to school before, of course - Charles always made sure I was on the school bus, when he could manage it. But a lot of the time he had to go to work before the school bus came, and my mother sure as hell wasn't putting me on it. She preferred to have me keeping her company, or fighting for money, or hustling. And she'd had a lifetime of experience in hiding from truant officers, starting when she was not much older than I was now.

So having the adult who runs the home *expect* me to go to school was pretty new. It was also terrifying.

I couldn't read. At all. Same for math. "2+2" meant the same thing to me that Sumerian cuneiform might mean to you.

I'd missed virtually all of first grade, and after that I always pretty much BSed being able to read and write on my short stints in public schools with Charles or my foster families. In public schools funded by the nonexistent property taxes on abandominiums and crack dens, most of my teachers were too overworked to do anything about it. Especially when Charles was never home and Nolita didn't care.

Aunt Patty cared.

"Hawk," she'd say, "don't you have homework?"

"Nah, Aunt Patty," I lied. "I already did it."

"Can I see it?"

"I mean, I did it in class. And turned it in before I came home."

Her eyebrow would go up, and I knew I was caught. Damn. I knew how hustlers hustled, how to dazzle a fiend, but I had no goddamn idea what to do with an adult who had the time and energy to care about my education.

"I look forward to seeing your report card, Hawk. They're sending them home in a few weeks."

How did you intercept a report card? I wasn't sure I knew what one looked like.

"Me too, Aunt Patty. I hope you'll be real proud."

☆☆☆

I am waiting for them when they open the door.

The school bathroom is a tight, confined space lined with dingy tiles. There's barely any room to move between the swinging stall doors and the sinks that jut out from the wall.

I'd rather do my fighting in a wide, open space. Like I was taught. In an alley, or in somebody's basement.

An alley would be wider than this. Grimier and darker, too with sharp corners instead of sinks. But it would at least be like back home.

I was a provider, back then. Good and powerful.

Everything is alien, here. Everything seems designed to lock me out.

But we don't always get to pick our battlefields. Here fighting isn't 'good,' but it's the only power I've got. Letters and papers on the page are impenetrable to me. I don't understand how power is wielded, here, or what makes these kids worlds go round.

The kids come in. Their clothes are new and crisp, the swinging of their arms innocent in a way I probably never was. By their age I'd seen kids shot by cops, kids my age slammed on the ground and dragged away.

Their carelessness, only makes me madder.

These kids have so much I do not. And worse, they despise *me* for it.

These are the kids who call me 'dumb.' Who make it clear

that I don't belong. Not in a real school, or in a neighborhood with nice houses and no gunshots. That I'll never be able to hold onto those things.

These kids have the round faces that come from always having enough to eat, the skinny little limbs that come from never having to rely on the strength of your arms to protect you. They can do magics I can't, but they are totally unprepared for what I *can* do.

They see me, but don't think I'm a threat. The gum-stained bathroom door swings harmlessly shut behind them, sealing us from view. One of them goes into a stall. The lock on the door will protect him.

I've seen kids OD. I've seen cops kill kids 'cause they thought they were carrying weapons, drag kids off to spend years in prison 'cause they were hustling drugs to feed their families. I've seen my stepdad walk up to the leanest, meanest hustler on the block and tell him to keep hands off my mother. These kids have no idea what I've seen.

I know I'm bigger than them, and I think about how intimidating I must look. I love and hate this thought at once. Love it because back home, power was a virtue and a necessity if you wanted to provide and protect. Hate it because it reminds me of the way my mother used to loom above me, grim and demanding, and tell scared six-year-old me that I'd better win this fight.

Am I becoming my mother? The father who I never saw because he was out, selling drugs and getting shot at by other hustlers?

I don't want to be here, in this world where power's found on pieces of paper I don't understand, and even kids act like I am worse than useless.

Back home, I was strong and skilled. I was a man.

But I don't want to be back there either. Not now that I've seen what's possible. That people like me can live in neighborhoods where bullets are not background noise and cops prevent crimes instead of committing them.

That's what these kids tell me, when they call me "dumb." They say 'you're going back there, and we're gonna laugh about it.'

Later I'll understand that they don't know. They don't know where I come from. They don't know what the world can be like for a kid of twelve years old, what it can ask him to do. They don't know to be afraid of me.

Later I'll understand that they're just kids, testing boundaries. That kids don't have to grow up so fast around here.

Today, all I know is that I'm on new turf. I've got to establish myself. To be on new turf and to let others push you around, where I come from, means death or slavery. Social power is the only kind of power we've got, and we sure as hell protect it.

I'm bigger than these other kids because I'm older. I can't read or write or do math, but there's one thing I can do better than anybody.

I never lost a fight back home. My neighbors called me their sure thing in a world of uncertainty. My strength, my skill with the clenched fist, was one of the only good things my neighborhood had going for it.

I'm not gonna kill these kids. I'm just gonna teach them a lesson.

I swing. The first kid goes down, shocked and easy. Blood

covers his face as his eyes go wide. He hits the tile floor, not knowing how to respond. I go to my knees on top of him and swing down. Two more punches ought to do it.

His friends run to get the teachers.

I look up at their retreating backs, and wish I knew what it was like to be able to run.

To have somebody to protect me.

☆☆☆

"Hawk," my Aunt Patty says, "you seem angry."

We're sitting in her son's red camaro in the driveway in front of her house. It's a nice house, in a nice neighborhood, with bushes and flowers carefully tended in the front.

I try to imagine somebody having the time to tend bushes and flowers. Having time to spend not just fighting to survive, and when they're not trying to get high. I see it every day while I live here, but I still don't understand it. Half of me thinks this is a movie set, all cardboard and staging, and one day I'm gonna come home from school to find that it has fallen down.

"Yeah."

That's about as much as I talk, these days. Nobody understands easily, and I wasn't taught to be good with words. I wasn't taught to be good with feelings. It's a bad combination. I say "yeah" a lot.

"Is there anything that I can do to help?"

I look at her. My aunt is about the prettiest lady you will ever see. Not 'sexy.' Pretty. She has skin the color of black coffee, a dignity and uprightness to her that I've never seen outside of television before. She wears bright colors, flowing outfits like robes that celebrate her body without advertising it. Like some sort of modern priestess. I try to imagine her walking down the street in my old neighborhood. I can't.

"Nah," I say. "It's - fine."

I could say 'I hate school.'

I could tell her that I can't make heads or tails of these numbers and letters, these things that other kids - *younger* kids - pick up and so easily make magic from.

I could tell her that I feel like these are some divine instructions that everybody hears except for me, and I'm convinced I'm not supposed to be here, but I'm also terrified of leaving.

I could tell her that, but I don't.

The way she looks at me makes me think she knows. Those eyes - sad, round, *kind* eyes. The kind of eyes you might see in a painting. Has anybody ever looked at me like that before? If so, I don't remember it.

I watch her bite her lip. Look away from me. I've never seen anybody do that before - control themselves like that. I've never seen anybody seem to just generally be in control of themselves.

Maybe she wants to say 'do you miss your mother,' or 'are you happy here?' Maybe she already knows the answers, knows that asking wouldn't help anybody. Instead, she gets out of the car.

I follow her into the house.

Today, Michael is playing with his robot toys, and Karlie is doing her homework.

I go to my room, where I spend my time getting lost in music.

A couple of years earlier, Charles gave me a boombox. It was my most prized possession, to the point that when foster care placed me with Patty, I made her take me back to Nolita's cockroach-ridden house to go get it. She had to wash it on the front porch 'cause she was scared that it had cockroach eggs in it, that her house would end up infested from it.

To me, that boombox was the world's most potent symbol of music.

Music is an escape. With music in your ears, beats flowing through your body, you feel alive in a way that isn't possible in silence. The music becomes something bigger than you - something real. And if you can become its conduit, you become something big and popular and glamorous too. You can become something with meaning and the power to heal.

That's why it's such a big deal in the hood. Music is an escape that you can package and sell without having to pay no Colombian supplier, an escape that won't get you arrested and sometimes, just sometimes, helps you make something of yourself instead of stopping you from living. Music was my dope.

I imagined walking up and down my block, boombox on my shoulder, bringing the joy and glory and vitality of music to everybody around me. I figured it would be a non-stop party: Hawk and his boombox, and everybody I passed by feeling good and dancing.

The only problem was, that boombox only actually worked for about a week.

I'm not sure what went wrong with it. We lost the power cord, or the batteries ran out, or some part of it broke, or *something.* It never worked after that. I didn't care. I was more interested in making sure the boombox stayed within my sight, that no one took it from me or messed with it in any way, than fixing it.

I had a boombox. Boomboxes were party machines. Mine *looked* like something that music was supposed to come out of, and that was enough.

Music comes from within, anybody will tell you. It lives in your brain and your blood, rattles around in there until it gets out somehow. Beats I'd heard on other people's radios lived in me just as clear as if my brain was a cassette, and I could play them back and make them come to life through my mouth and my body, through dance. I don't know how many hours I spent, me and that boombox, jamming out to silence.

I dreamed, vividly, of paradise. Paradise, to me, looked like:

Walking up and down the block. Right where I lived now, but free and easy. Arms swinging in the breeze, taking in the sunlight, throwing my cares to the wind as I embraced the world.

In my dream, the boombox worked. I carried music with me everywhere I went. Beats - a thing recognizably of the hood, of the streets, but also glamorous, successful. Basketball and music were the only validation we got; the only time we saw people like us becoming successful and recognized as good with the kinds of skills we could afford to cultivate.

So in my dream I carried this boombox around, bringing

beats, bringing the energy and joy, everywhere I went. To pace the block without a worry was to rule it. In my dream, I still swept barbershop floors - but I was so successful at it that I was doing them a favor and not the other way around.

In my dream I was known. Respected. Liked. Not for beating up other defenseless kids for money, but for the gifts of music and ease. I was a hustler of the only things that struck me as good, Rhythm and Poetry. I was respected the same as the hustlers of the real stuff, the stuff that moved tens of thousands of dollars of other people's money, the kind of money that people like my mother could only dream of.

In my dream, I was a provider. Not of crack money, but of music.

☆☆☆

Sitting in the bright, clean school principal's office with my aunt is about the most scared I've ever been. Scarier than underground fighting matches with blood in my eyes. Scarier than hiding from the cops in crackhouses.

It's scarier because she's my aunt. She is an angel and a saint and if anybody had ever proposed to me that Jesus could be a woman, I'd think she was that, too. She is everything I've ever thought I couldn't have, and she's nice to me.

If I was afraid to disappoint my mother, I am *terrified* to disappoint my aunt.

So my heart is pounding and my palms are sweating as this big, fat, principal guy in a suit says: "Mrs. Williams, we've called you here because we think Hawk should be placed in one of our special education classes."

I didn't know at the time what that meant. What I knew was that anything a fat guy in a suit wanted to do related to me was bad, bad, bad.

My aunt straightens in her seat. Crosses her arms. "Excuse me?"

"Well, Mrs. Williams," the principle fidgets.

My aunt has this way about her that can make a grown man fidget. Make someone who's supposed to be in charge fidget like a little kid who has been bad. I love her for it.

"Hawk can't read. The boy is twelve years old and he shows no apparent understanding of the alphabet, or of numbers. Our regular teachers, to be frank, can't help him."

"Then your teachers," she says, with that soft, here-comes-the-sentencing voice, "are not doing their job."

"Mrs. Williams, has Hawk been asking for help with his homework...at home?"

She looked at me and I know I was in trouble. But I also know that somehow, so is the principal. That considerably brightens my outlook on the situation.

"I'll help him," my aunt says, her dark eyes sparkling, "at home. But let me tell you, this child is not disabled. I watch him every day. He's as smart as any of my other children."

Hearing her say that kind of made my head spin. No one in my life has ever told me I'm smart, much less said it when I'm in trouble for not having turned in a single piece of homework in the past semester.

Plus, *other children*. Not a foster kid, not a charity case, not a temporary nuisance. One of *her children*.

My aunt's hand is on my shoulder then, gentle. "Let's go, Hawk."

I stand up, glad to be out of there. Especially because my eyes are burning and I am *not* going to let this man in a suit see me cry.

We leave the office, my aunt standing tall and me feeling like I've unwittingly won some kind of victory.

☆☆☆

Aunt Patty sent me to Sylvan for remedial math and reading lessons. She also made Karlie help me with my homework, which made Karlie mad as a chained pit bull.

"But Mooom," she'd protest, "I already did *my* homework."

"Yes, Karlie. But Hawk is family, and he needs your help."

"But Mooom…"

Patty's eyebrows would go up, and Karlie would fall into line.

I didn't love having my free time taken up taking instructions from a little girl, either. But I had to admit, Karlie was *damn* smart. She'd start out just trying to help me spell a three-letter word, and end up explaining things to me that I'm pretty sure my teachers didn't know.

"This textbook's wrong. See, they say Watson and Crick discovered the double helix structure of DNA, but they actually used the work of this woman named Rosalind Franklin to do it. Franklin had taken these special pictures of the DNA molecule, called X-ray crystallography, and they saw the pictures while visiting her lab one day."

I listened, nodding. "So is that what I should write on this paper?"

"Sure. If you want to."

"...Karlie?"

"Yeah?"

"What's DNA?"

Slow comprehension dawns on Karlie's face. "Oh my God. You can't read, can you?"

"I can read...some."

"DNA. How do you spell D-N-A?"

In hindsight, I realize she was saying the letters. But back in the day, what I heard was a word pronounced "dee-en-ay," and I had no idea how that was spelled.

"Well see, this is the letter called 'D'. It makes the 'duh' sound."

For my part, I am almost ashamed to, secretly, be working *hard* at school for the first time in my life. Hustlers didn't respect school, didn't waste energy on it.

But hustlers weren't Aunt Patty, and by then I admired her more.

☆☆☆

"I can't compete with your love."

I didn't hear my mother say this to my aunt. I didn't hear the terrible, desperate conversation where she said this.

We'd been separated for two years, by that time, and I had almost forgotten about life with my mother. She was now a ghost who faded in and out of my life, who sometimes called, who sometimes complained about not being allowed to see me. I did what she asked, when she asked with that tone in her voice like the look she gave me at the fighting ring matches. But having seen the other side of the fence, I no longer *wanted* to live with her.

I was too ashamed of this thought to admit it. But I felt it. I felt anxiety at the thought of Nolita, of sleeping with her curled up on the living room floor by candlelight. I felt it in the way my pulse pounded when I thought of the fight clubs, of being told to split another child's face open.

I didn't know what to do with that feeling so I just tried, quietly, to forget that things had ever been any other way. I was one of Patty's children now. I went to school. I was reading at a third grade level. I had a warm, safe home and crazy smart siblings who had my back like no street gang ever had.

I was one of Patty's children. I had a future. My mother knew it.

"I remember," my mother said to Aunt Patty, "how you've always been the only one working for me. The only one fighting for me. Trying to protect me. The only one getting me out of jail when I fell. I can't compete with your love.

"And I don't want you to steal my son from me."

That was Nolita's apology and her declaration of war, all in one.

I didn't know about the war. I didn't know social services did everything they could to keep me away from my mother. I didn't know that that was why I wasn't allowed to have a house key - because if I did, they knew, I'd let my mother into my Aunt Patty's house. And no one knew what would happen then.

I didn't know that that was why my mother told me to lie.

I talked to my mother on the phone every week or two. The anger hadn't set in yet. I knew that she was my mother, and that she treated me as her best friend. I was her little man, her baby, her forever friend. That was why she used to take me everywhere with her. That was why she relied on me so much.

I knew my mother needed me.

I fought to get my mother money. I went with her to the crack houses, because she couldn't bear to be without me. I kept quiet when I was with her and my stepdad came looking, banging on the door and hollering for his Nolita. I did whatever my mother told me to do.

My mother knew best. So when my mother asked me to lie, in one of our weekly phone calls, I knew it was the right thing to do.

"Tell your social worker," she said, "that Patty locks you out of the house. Tell them you were sitting in the freezing cold because she wouldn't let you in."

I told my social worker, the next time I saw her. But the neighbors joined Patty to refute the story. Under pressure, I told the truth: no, that hadn't really happened. My mother told me I should say it.

"Tell your social worker," my mother said, "that Patty's son - the big one, what's his name?"

"Phillip."

"Tell her Phillip hit you."

It was true, technically. My rambunctious energy had been been rubbing off on Karlie and Michael, and once the three of us, together, managed to put a television clear through one of the walls of Aunt Patty's beautiful house.

As the plaster crumbled into dust on the carpet, Aunt Patty declared that this could not go on any longer. We would all be disciplined the same: a spanking for Michael, one for Karlie, one for me. I was the biggest of the three, and the most violently resistant; so Phillip helped.

That one took.

Phillip and Patty could not honestly deny that he had put his hands on me. That it was at his mother's request, and to enforce the same discipline she administered to her own children, did not make a difference.

I wanted to say something. That Aunt Patty and Phillip were wonderful. That a spanking was nothing compared to the foster homes I had been in before. That I did not, really, want to go back to my mother.

But my mother needed me. She had given me instructions. I could not disappoint my mother.

The social workers said this couldn't happen again. That no one could spank me, no matter what I did. Today, we know that spanking only makes kids angrier, only make them behave worse. But all Patty knew was that they were asking her to treat me different from her other kids.

And it got worse. Because he had been involved, the social workers explained, Phillip would have to be fingerprinted. A file would have to be created for him, in the system.

Patty knew what disaster that could spell for a young black man with a promising career. Phillip was on the verge of graduating with honors, on the verge of being accepted to his choice of several prestigious business internships.

"You will not fingerprint my son," she said. "No employer will do a background check, and find a record on him. Least of all a record of alleged child abuse."

"Then Hawk can't stay here."

"But I've already started proceedings to adopt him as my own child - I was told that those proceedings were almost complete. Is that not true?"

"The paperwork's a month or two from being finished. But we can't place him in a home - foster or adoptive - if we can't show that we have taken all appropriate steps to verify his safety. We can't let him stay here in either capacity unless we create a file on your son."

My aunt Patty looked at Phillip. He was close, so close to making it. To making the kind of career that can lift a family, jump the divide between the classes in America. The kind of career that can raise a gaggle of kids with access to the best schools, to the kind of tutors that will get them even higher up the ladder.

I was putting televisions through walls, and lying to the social services.

Patty started to cry.

Then, she did what Aunt Patty did best: she got shit done.

She started to make phone calls. She started to do paperwork. My grandmother, my father's mother, had a reasonably good home in one of the better parts of the ghetto. But because she was blood family, the state would not give her money to help her care for me. And she was already stretched to the limit of her nurse's paycheck: she cared for two young children, sons of her drug-addicted nieces.

"What if," Patty proposed, "I could find a way for them to pay you."

She set out to make it so. She somehow found the right forms, talked to the right people, made it possible for my grandmother to receive the payments that would allow her to support me and continue my education.

When everything was in order, my social worker told Patty it was time.

"I can't tell him," Patty said with tears in her eyes. "I can't tell him that he can't come home. You take him. I'll give you his things. Pick him up from school, and tell him he's going to his grandmother's house."

☆☆☆

There are no words for what I felt when my social worker's car pulled up. There was a plastic trash bag in the back of it. That was where they always put foster kids' stuff when they were moving homes: there was no budget for suitcases, so everything essential went into a garbage bag, and went into the back seat with you.

I was in a daze as I walked to the car. My teacher had held me back as the school day ended, he told me to wait for a car instead of getting on the bus. He hadn't told me why. I think that was when my mind blanked. I couldn't think of any scenarios that were good ones, so I didn't think of any at all.

Time seemed to move in slow motion as I walked from where I'd waited with my teacher, pulled on the car door handle and swung myself inside. I sat in the back seat, silent, staring.

"Hawk," my social worker said with false cheerfulness. "We've got - some exciting news for you! You're gonna go stay with your grandmother now!"

I did not think to ask why. If I'd been paying attention to what Patty told me, not blinding myself with the idea that my mother would never do anything bad, I'd have already known.

Patty had tried to explain to me, more than once, what would happen if the state deemed her house unsafe for me. But I'd shoved it all to the back of my mind. I fantasized that maybe my mother was getting better, that maybe she'd soon have Charles and the kids back when she told me to tell them that Patty's son hit me.

So now, I didn't make any connection between what I'd said, what I'd done, or the garbage bag full of my clothes in the back of the car. I thought Patty must have decided that she didn't want me anymore.

I didn't say anything, and I didn't cry, as the car started to move.

☆☆☆

THE ALL-STAR

I go heart and soul in them streets

Heart and soul in these beats

I'm gonna make sure we gonna eat

I go in so in love wit them streets

Niggas hating feels like the devil waiting on me

Lord please help me I ain't slept in weeks

My grandmother's house was respectable. Warm, sparse, clean. It was all greys and whites. Clean, efficient, and serviceable, but never bold or gaudy.

That just about describes my grandmother too. She was caring and supportive, but also stern, modest, no-nonsense. A single, middle-aged woman who worked as a nurse, she was already raising two kids who were younger than me.

I would later learn that Aunt Patty had called her up and begged her to take me in when she learned that I could not stay with her. My grandmother had stressed about how she didn't have money to care for herself *and* three children, but Aunt Patty had somehow pulled some strings and found a way to get my grandmother a foster parent stipend for me, even though we were related by blood which would normally make her ineligible.

All I knew at the time was that this was my new home.

I'd often visited my grandmother when I was with my mother or Aunt Patty. I liked her well enough, and her home already felt a little bit like home to me.

But I missed Karlie, Michael and Aunt Patty fiercely. I missed my mother too, though by now I'd tasted enough of safety and stability to know that I didn't really want to go live with her again.

I went to school - I would have been changing schools that year anyway, as I'd finished out my middle school with Aunt Patty and graduated, just barely, into high school. And the move put me in the same district as Jordan - my brother, not by blood, but in every way that counted.

Jordan lived in my grandmother's neighborhood, so I'd met him as a young kid visiting family. To an outsider, we were as different as two black boys from the hood could possibly be. He was educated, book-smart, rich by local standards - his mother lived in the best part of town that could still be properly called 'the hood' and sent him to a private school where he was the only black student.

The other kids didn't fully know what to do with him - he didn't quite fit in, had less street cred and street smarts than anyone else, would have been a ripe target for bullying on both the street and his all-white private school if things had been just a little different.

But he had this natural charisma and calm that somehow made him a leader of the pack anyway. Somehow he turned his book smarts from a liability into an asset, turned the discipline he was subjected to at school into leadership ability.

Whenever a fight went too far, it was Jordan who broke it up. When somebody lost their shit, it was Jordan who cooled them down. His way with people plus his unusual degree of wealth and class gave him almost a sort of fairy-tale-prince mystique, like he was some kind of minor nobility that made other kids just naturally look to him for guidance.

I was coming from the opposite end of the spectrum. My grandmother's house was close enough to Nolita's neighborhood that most everyone knew my reputation. I was the certified with street cred - a champion, a hustler, a dude with connections. At fourteen, I was practically considered an OG. But I was undisciplined and hotheaded as shit. Living by street rules meant that every minor disrespect had to be dealt with swiftly and decisively, with fists and fury, lest somebody decide you were an easy mark and escalate a war against you.

This didn't translate so well on the local basketball court.

That might be what brought us together. When I lost my shit, Jordan calmed me down. And I recognized a good thing when I saw it: I recognized Jordan as a good thing.

Soon after meeting, we learned that we were complementary in more ways than one. I had a biological dad who was a hustler, who I'd never really known; so did Jordan. I had a mother in the deepest depths of drug addiction; he had a mother who struggled not to fall into it, haunted by memories and former contacts from that world.

His mom had managed to stay off the stuff, to get a good lawyer and a good divorce settlement when her husband left her for the street life. Now she lived like minor royalty up on the hill, a mysterious, distant, dignified figure. But Jordan's fears and mine were the same: what would become of our mothers, if we couldn't support them?

The other kids in our crew never saw that side of us. The face we presented to the world - first separately and then together - was the face of the ultimate cool kids. Between us, we knew everything there was for a kid to know. Jordan knew rich kids and rich kid things; I knew OGs and hustlers, local celebrities. We were a dynamic duo, leading our crew to glorious success.

That success, eventually, had to involve hustling.

I mentioned that my grandmother didn't have much: that was really true. When it came to clothes, we made due with the most efficient possible options. It was thrift stores and charity, clothes worn until they were falling apart or too damn small to fit. Forget about allowances, disposable income, and fun. My grandmother was, by necessity, very serious and focused on survival.

Unfortunately, that sort of spelled social death in hood circles at that time.

Idolizing OGs had led to a culture of conspicuous consumption. In other words, you showed how badass you were by buying the best clothes, shoes, jewelry, cars. Lots of kids couldn't afford much, but it was assumed that anyone who really had their act together should look like it. Showing up in bullshit thrift store clothes told people you didn't have your shit together.

Too young for a legal job, I knew one way to fix the situation.

Getting back into hustling was so easy. It was like all I had to do was set foot in the old hood and people mobbed me. "Hawk, where you been? Hawk, we been looking for you!"

The OGs were all dying to have my street smarts, my strategic mind, my inherent *responsibleness* back in the game. Within a week, I was cooking and distributing. Within two weeks, I was rolling in the dough.

With dough came bling. I hadn't lost my sense of self-preservation - most of my money still went into savings. But I also got fly jackets, the best shoes, just enough jewelry to show status without showing off, and, eventually, a sports car. And - as is often true of hustlers - what was mine was also my crew's. While I had cash, nobody in my crew was gonna look shabby or be without a smooth ride.

By tenth grade, our crew was known everywhere. Girls and athletes tripped over themselves for invitations to hang out with us. At the local skating rink, the staff all knew us, the regulars all knew us. We just had to walk in the door and it was 'they're here!'

We even became popular at the local college. To explain where we were getting our income, my crew and I got jobs working in the cafeteria of the nearby college as soon as we turned 16. There, we delighted in smooth-talking the female students and never, ever told anybody how old we were. We drove up to work in our new sports cars - only the best for my crew - so they assumed we couldn't be high school kids.

From the age of 16 on, we only dated college women, and got invited to all the best college parties.

I was also a star athlete long enough for people to remember me that way. The seriousness I'd learned to put into fighting translated brilliantly into football. I was good. Like, 'athletic scholarship' good.

Unfortunately, my sports career was brief.

Between the hustling and the job I worked to cover for it, I was effectively working two jobs while attending school full-time. Job #1, job #2, sports, school - something had to go.

By junior year, it was the sports. My reputation had been established among local kids, but I'd never get athletic scholarships, never play for a college football team. Outside of school, every spare minute was split between business - and the parties that were the sweet fruit of that businesses.

Given my hustling-and-partying lifestyle, it might surprise you to hear that I was well-liked by teachers. My most valuable skill, like Jordan's, was my skill with people. Just like he'd survived childhood in the hood on people skills alone, I got through high school the same way.

I didn't spend much time or energy on schoolwork. But I respected teachers, even if I didn't learn from them. I took care of problems that came up among the student body, and the teachers knew it. I played big brother to other students just like I was big brother to my own siblings and the kids hustling on my block. As far as the teachers were concerned, if I didn't do my homework, it was because I was taking care of more important things.

The teachers knew the community. The teachers understood.

I graduated high school at nineteen. My ever-growing hustling empire meant there was no financial need for me to go to college or get a legal job - I could have lived well, become an OG, a respected authority figure. I picked fewer fights and exercised enough restraint that I would probably even live past thirty.

But I knew that something was wrong.

I'd seen what drugs had done to my mother. I'd seen what they did to countless people, as a hustler. Whether you were buying or selling, eventually they got you. You wind up dead from an overdose, get lung problems from smoking, get shot by a rival or a hustler you don't pay, or get trapped behind bars for life.

I had also seen a better world through my time spent with Aunt Patty and the rich people's events I went to with Jordan through his school. I'd seen black people with nice houses and college degrees. I'd seen respected black professionals and black genius kids at the top of their class in fancy private schools. I'd seen black people achieve these things without any involvement with drugs.

I'd seen rich men with white hair - *old* men who gave their kids a future that didn't involve addiction, incarceration, or getting shot at.

Hustling had seemed like a good idea when I was too young to work legally, stuck in school full-time with a grandmother who had little to give me.

But now I was free. My high school diploma meant that I could go to college if I wanted to, get a full-time legal job if I wanted to. It meant I was an adult, responsible for my own future and my community, in the eyes of the state as well as the neighborhood.

As a hustler, I wasn't living up to my own standards, my ambitions, to what I knew to be right.

There had to be a better way.

CRIMINAL JUSTICE

Young boys, they squeezing triggers wit no hesitation
Running thru these streets blind, wit no education
They not thinking 'bout the jail they got waiting
10 years with a plea bargain, take it
Now you sitting in the cell and u gotta face it
Picking up a rag, join a gang ya may make it
Then u realize u not tuff so u fake it
It's a war inside, dey stripping niggas naked

Of all the people in the hood, in the whole world, I was probably the last one you'd expect to be a prison guard. But three years out of high school, the high roller who used to buy cocaine in bulk and cook crack for whole neighborhoods was doing just that. It made a weird amount of sense.

After high school, I started looking for a legit job that would neither starve me nor make me miserable.

I came damn close to joining the military. The benefits looked great, and the career advancement paths they offered for recruits who scored high on aptitude tests were awesome. The military had structure and prestige. It was where my Grandad had made a name for himself.

But something in me didn't feel right about that. Sure, the military was great to my grandfather. It was great for lots of people. But I'd always done better on the streets than in school because I was an independent thinker, someone who solved problems without being asked and didn't have much interest in being told what to do. Would the military be good for *that*?

I stared at the last form they sent me to begin the sign-up process, folded it, and put it in my desk drawer. No military for me. At least, not yet.

I tried working in a warehouse, a job that promised legit, full-time pay. "Full-time pay" turned out to be terrible pay - I could barely keep a roof over my head and the most basic of foods in the fridge, never mind putting any away into savings or investments.

I got a job at the local post office. The pay was decent, but the work was not enough to keep my mind occupied. Some part of me was always solving problems, asking questions, wanting to make a difference. Not a lot of opportunity for that in a job based on routine. I have mad respect for the folks who make mail deliveries happen - but I couldn't do it.

A cousin of mine had enrolled in a nearby technical college, studying construction skills that he said would get him a bigger paycheck than any unskilled labor. I got my own certification in electrical construction - that is, wiring up new houses while they're being built - but quickly found that that also made me miserable, especially with the way contractors tended to treat their workers like they didn't know anything.

Finally, I found an ad for a job that had good pay, good benefits, was completely legal, and seemed like it required my unique skill set.

The ad was for a Maryland State Prison correctional officer.

The state takes care of its prison guards pretty good. It has to. The work is demanding, sensitive, and downright dangerous. In that field, sometimes, even doing your job exactly right isn't enough to keep from getting your head cracked open.

So there were great health benefits. A workers' comp policy which promised you'd be salaried for a whole year if you were hurt on the job and unable to work. Good hourly pay - the kind of pay that would convince a man to do work in a job where he could get shanked instead of in a warehouse.

I took it.

And, admittingly, being a correctional officer felt like being around my people. The people I was supposed to be with. This was because so many of the people I had grown up with were now incarcerated.

These people respected me. They knew me. And I respected them. Neither of us liked the fact that they were locked up here, but they understood that that's just how things were. It wasn't like I, personally, was running the courts and the prison system.

And it wasn't like they were bad people.

In those days, getting caught with five grams of crack would get you anywhere between five to forty years in prison. A paper-clip weighs about a gram, so imagine how much five paper-clips weigh. You didn't even have to be a hustler to get what was effectively a life sentence for drug possession. No violent offenses were necessary. In a lot of places, that hasn't changed much to this day.

And then there were all the people who were in for other offenses. Sometimes they were in for assault or battery - sometimes for settling disputes in the usual street way, with fists. Sometimes for mugging passersby for crack money - I'd never done that, but my mother had. Sometimes for just being in the wrong place at the wrong time and getting mistaken for someone else. Police seemed to have a lot of trouble telling black and brown males apart.

But it was the way it was. If anything, the guys appreciated working with me. I respected them as no high-and-mighty-out-of-the-suburbs guard ever would. I knew them, and I knew their needs, and lots of them had seen me tend to their family's needs on the outside.

I don't think I was as happy with the situation as they were.

I noticed something weird right away, from the first day I was on the job. Why were damn near all the prisoners black?

I'd spent most of my youth around drugs on the streets. I knew who used them. White people, black people, Hispanic people, Asian people. Everybody. My own hood was mostly black, but lots of white folks visited the hood specifically to buy their drugs. Lots of the Plugs - the guys the OGs got their whole bricks from - were white. They were rich white guys, moving more quantity than the OGs ever did. Moving it, probably, both into urban communities and corporate boardrooms.

So why was it only the black hustlers and users I saw in Maryland State?

It bothered me to no end. It bothered me so much that I started looking up ways I could learn why this was the way it was, and how I could do something about it. I ended up in a Criminal Justice degree program at Baltimore City Community College, taking classes a few at a time around my day job as a correctional officer.

The more I learned in my Criminal Justice classes, the more pissed off I got.

I learned, that possession of crack cocaine was punished 100 times harder than possession of the powdered stuff. Getting caught with a few paperclips' weight in crack would get you ten years. To get the same sentence for possession of powder, you'd need to be caught with a briefcase full.

Of course, it was obvious why. Powdered cocaine was the glamorous drug of A-list movie stars, Wall Street bankers, and anyone white folks wanted to pretend to be. Crack was seen as the devil's drug, for no reason I could discern except that it was cheaper, so it attracted more black hustlers and users.

I eventually learned that one of Richard Nixon's advisors had straight-up said as much to a journalist: that the laws that started the "war on drugs" in the 60s were made to allow the government to arrest blacks and hippies, because the government was afraid of those groups organizing.

I discovered that was the reason why powdered cocaine - already the drug of rich white folks in the 60s - was barely punished, while the crack that was popular in black neighborhoods at that time could land you instant life in prison if the cops decided they wanted to bring you in. For a few years, they hit the hippie community the same way: first-time marijuana possession had a minimum mandatory sentence of two to ten years in prison.

The government apparently lost its fear of hippies and repealed the minimum of two years in prison for marijuana possession in the 70s. But at the same time they actually made crack punishments harsher.

I could understand why you'd want cocaine to be illegal. Having known my mother, I understood better than anybody how it destroyed a person's soul. But anybody with eyes could see that putting hustlers away for ten years for nonviolent crimes was only making things worse. It was only making it harder for people like my mother to get help, or jobs, and for kids raised in the hood to have a future. It divided families and started generational curses that carry broken legacies. If I had at any point been arrested during my hustling career, my life would've been gone.

The sentencing differences for crack explained some of why there were almost no white guys in Maryland State. Get picked up for crack, you stay in ten times longer than a guy who gets picked up for powdered coke.

But it didn't explain all of it. I knew that cops decided who to arrest almost randomly: they knew where I hustled, they knew *that* I hustled, but they decided not to pick me up. If they'd arrested everyone doing or selling crack, my whole neighborhood would've been gone. That just wasn't practical.

So how, I wondered, did they decide who to arrest? It wasn't based on who had drugs. It was based on who had drugs, *and* who the cops wanted locked up. What determines that?

I learned that Maryland state wasn't unique: prisons around the country were filled with black people. Which might've just made me think that black people were criminals if I didn't *know* criminals so well. I knew criminals came in all colors, and that rich white dudes moved more coke than anyone. And the white dudes who did those things were all mysteriously missing from this prison.

The more I learned and the more I thought, the less I liked

my job.

People ending up behind bars for drugs was no longer just 'how things worked.' I now saw that it almost only happened to people who looked like me. Not to rich white connects. Not to rich white customers. Just us.

Although I grew to hate my job - looking every day into the faces of men who I was pretty sure should not have been there - I had no plans to quit until I finished my degree and could get a better profession. This time maybe somewhere where I could make a difference.

But it didn't go that smoothly.

You'd think with everything I've been through, that if I was gonna end up disabled it would be in some kind of dramatic way. You'd think I would get shot or stabbed or beaten up in some prison yard fight.

But it was a goddamn slippery step that changed the course of my life. And it was the prisoners who protected me.

Every day for one hour, they'd let the prisoners out into the yard. They'd exercise, play basketball. That hour a day was precious - and required by law - so it was pretty difficult to get rained out.

Out in the courtyard was one little guard house. It was more of a shack than a building, just four walls, a roof, and some really thick glass. That was where I stood when I was on duty to watch them. For the most part, prisoners avoided that house, and I avoided them unless they were obviously fixing to kill each other.

One day it started to rain. It was more like just getting a bucket of water dumped on your head than rain. Having a bunch of convicts turned loose in blinding rain was a bad idea, so me and the other guards moved to bring them inside.

The guard house had a couple of old wooden steps leading down from the door onto concrete. As I ran to round up the inmates, the wet wood broke under my foot.

The Next thing I remember, I woke up in an ambulance with agonizing pain in my head and shoulder. I tried to move and found out my right arm was sticking out at a funny angle. Shit.

At the hospital, the doctor told me concrete is the devil. Fall and hit your head on concrete, even just from standing height, and you can be looking at a fatal brain injury. I'd been lucky. It could have been much worse. But still, I'd had three seizures before waking up in the ambulance.

Later, I found out, the other guards hadn't even seen me go down. They couldn't see where I'd fallen from any of the cameras, didn't know anything was wrong. I'd been alone and unconscious, in the open yard with the inmates. They could easily have killed me.

Instead, they picked me up. They made sure I didn't hit my head on the concrete anymore as the seizures tore through me. Some of them ran to the other guards for help. The guards came running and called the ambulance.

On this day, the inmates guarded me. It was like I'd said from the beginning: they weren't bad people.

They were just unlucky.

THE OPEN ROAD

Whatcha know 'bout the hood boy?
I'm from a place where
There ain't nothing good boy

Ain't no good schools
Ain't no good markets
Ain't no good jobs
We just targets

When I first heard about truck driver salaries, I thought it was too good to be true. Everybody thinks of that as a shit job - which I learned after a while is true. But not because it's easy. Because it's so damn hard.

I couldn't be a correctional officer anymore after my head got busted up. I tried, and the system tried to make it work, but my injuries were pretty bad.

Most of it was my brain. They put me on workers' comp for eleven and a half months while doctors and therapists tried to do something about the migraines that would leave me unable to see properly, let alone focus on what was in front of me. That was no kind of trait for a prison guard, especially when the condition was triggered by stress. It didn't help that my ability to handle fights was also shot, with my shoulder getting wrenched out of its socket and being surgically put back together after the fall.

After eleven and a half months, they tried assigning me to a women's prison. They hoped the women would be easier to deal with. It didn't make any difference. I was not somebody who should be working in a dangerous environment. The state medically retired me, declaring me unsuited to any hard labor job.

The truck company offered to pay me almost what I made previously - if I passed their driving certification. Those gigantic cabs felt more like flying an airplane than driving a car. But driving was always something I'd been good at.

There were weird parts of the job that I was good at, too. Parts of the job nobody tells you about.

My job as a trucker was basically to move lots of stuff across the country so it could be sold in stores, as fast as possible. I had experience with routes and schedules that were modeled around getting the stuff from point A to point B as you could.

Driving long distances was alien to me. Baltimore is huge in terms of people, small in terms of distance. So many people stacked on top of each other, so many different neighborhoods, so many cultures and races and income levels all crammed with in the city limits. It feels like there are worlds within worlds in the city. You could probably live here your whole life without ever fully knowing your way around, let alone running out of new places to go.

But all of Baltimore is crammed into an area that's about ten miles on each side. Twenty miles was a really long distance. I was shocked to learn that Los Angeles was 2,500 miles away. Even more to learn that you could drive there and back in a week.

The first time I got into my truck to do a long route, it was amazing. Some part of my brain kept expecting the road to just *stop*, or loop back in on itself. I'd been told I had to drive for three days to get to LA, but about three hours into the drive I started feeling like I should be there already - I was already further from home than I'd been in my entire life.

Then I started thinking about what that three days of driving really meant.

I drove along these crazy roads with sharp turns and sharper drop-offs through the mountains in Pennsylvania that looked like something off of postcards. More trees than I ever knew existed, let alone just in the next state over from my home.

I drove between these huge farmer's fields all through the midwest, where little baby plants that were gonna be corn or alfalfa or just plain grass were growing flat practically to the horizon. I never knew there was so much open land right here in America, while people were living on top of each other in Baltimore.

The fields seemed to go on forever. *Literally* for days. Ohio, Illinois, Missouri, Oklahoma. Here and there there were little patches of forest, but nothing like the New England mountains.

Things started to get really crazy when I got to the southwest. It was just like you'd see in movies. The ground getting too dry for much grass to grow, red and dusty with weird little squat trees and bushes growing out in places. *Weird* landmarks like striped red-and-white cliffs sticking straight up out of the dirt like somebody took a birthday cake slice out of the Earth and dropped it there.

Herds of cows. Old-school, dusty, southern cattle. Not the fat, clean, black-and-white dairy cows I'd been seeing all across the midwest. I started to wonder if cowboy movies were still happening out here!

By the time I finally rolled into California, my mind was blown. The world - hell, just the United States - was so much bigger than I'd ever thought it could be. What happened in the small towns in those crazy green mountains, in the little farm houses off the highway, on those honest-to-God desert cattle ranches?

What kinds of lives were those people living?

Just like seeing Aunt Patty's nice house and the rich old men at Jordan's school had blown my mind. This really made me think about how few opportunities kids from my hood got to see. We didn't really even know what life was like in the rich neighborhoods, let alone in the Alleghenies or the Corn Belt or the Sonoran desert.

I'd had a teacher, once, in high school, who said that "books were windows to other worlds." I was starting to wonder what would've happened if I'd grown up reading those books instead of studying the streets.

I rolled into LA exhausted. Driving eleven hours per day took more out of me than I'd expected - but apparently I handled it better than most. Lots of truckers, I heard, dropped out of the game after their first few months. That was why the pay was so good - lots of people just couldn't take it.

I thought it was cool to live in my own private little room. A trucker's truck becomes more home than any motel room or even apartment. It's tiny, but it's *yours* to do whatever the hell you want with and take wherever you please. There's a kind of power in being able to take your home with you wherever you want. After a while, it doesn't really matter much if that home is damn tiny.

As part of its training program, the truck company had what was basically a barracks for its truckers outside of Waxahachie, Texas. We each got a little room on this compound outside of town, by a huge semi truck parking lot where courses and road tests were given. We lived there between assignments - not a lot of point in trying to live anywhere else, when time between assignments was usually only a few days, and Waxahachie was the hub of the truck company's routes.

Most of us didn't actually have cars down there. We'd driven the trucks in, and when we weren't using them we were on foot. Me and a bunch of other truckers would sometimes take the long walk from our little rooms on the outskirts into Waxahachie proper.

Waxahachie is about as far from Baltimore as you can get while still living in the same country.

I mean that in terms of *what* the city is - not just where it is. It's a small town with about 30,000 people in it, mostly living in these cute little old-style buildings that sprawl out across long miles of green grass. Somebody at some point called Waxahachie "The Gingerbread City" because some of its buildings are made out of these bricks and stones that are the same bright red-orange color as the desert around it. When you put white trim on them, they really do look like storybook drawings of houses made out of gingerbread with icing around the windows and doors.

Lots of the buildings have old-fashioned architecture too, with lots of little arches and round windows and white trim. It makes the whole place feel like it's some sort of fairy tale world or old west movie set.

The people of Waxahachie were almost entirely white, and

everybody had a suntan because they were outside all the time. They were also so friendly it was almost like being in my own hood. There, people were friendly because they knew you. Here, people were friendly because they *didn't*, and there were few enough new faces around that that made you kind of special.

I didn't spend much time in Waxahachie, but there was something important about living there for a little while. Something important about spending my days wandering around on green grass in a place that felt like it came straight out of a cowboy novel instead of surrounded by concrete and the press of people. I missed my hood, but at the same time I resented it a little bit. There was so much of life it hadn't shown me -so much it didn't show the kids growing up there.

I wondered what my mother's life would have been like if she'd grown up in a place like this.

Seeing the country, living in Waxahachie, gave me something new. It wasn't that Waxahachie was better than Baltimore. It was such a small city in part because there weren't enough jobs to support 600,000+ people like Baltimore, and the people there didn't really understand how life was for people in the big cities.

They didn't see the use of programs like Medicaid that allowed me and my siblings to survive growing up, and they didn't know what the drug war really was. They'd never lived in neighborhoods where the schools were so bad and life expectancies so short that drugs were seen as the only viable industry. They hadn't sold drugs to white folks and black folks alike - and then watched only the black folks end up in prison.

They were really kind to me, figuring I was a respectable,

hard-working guy since I had enough money to move to their community. But the way they saw the world was so different from the way I saw it. I wished there were some way they could understand the things they hadn't seen.

I drove for the truck company for almost a year - but I soon learned how hard it was.

Driving is easy. Until you've been doing it for eight hours straight. And then for *days* straight. And then doing that for weeks, barely seeing another living soul, no company except for the people you pass in truck stops along the way.

There are few lasting relationships there. Everybody's always on different routes. You almost never see the same trucker twice unless you go out of your way to work something out. It's no way to make friends. Ninety-percent of the time you're as alone as a person can get, just you and the rig and miles and miles of land ahead of you.

It was refreshing for a while. But I see now why being a trucker in the long term is so hard. Why it pays so well, to try to keep people from quitting.

For folks who like to keep to themselves, I imagine the freedom could be pretty great. It did help me sort my head out - being away from the hustle and demands of my hood helped me figure out who I was, and who I was not. Who I wanted to be, versus who they expected me to be.

But I'd always been a people person, and without anybody to talk to for days on end, some days I felt like I was gonna start talking to the trees and crickets in the grass.

After about eight months of driving all around this grand old country, I had my head sorted out. I was ready to make my next move.

And that was going to require some strategy.

THE HIGH LIFE

I love the fast cars and money, I don't know no better
The streets made me crazy with what they showed me
Now I'm selling all these drugs, yea I'm serving fiends
So I can afford the things I see in magazines
In reality a nigga living pipe dreams

Jordan and I wanted to get out of the drug game. But to make the money we needed to start a legit business, we had to get back into it first. So we compromised: instead of crack, we'd sell marijuana.

These days everybody knows weed is less addictive than cigarettes and harder to overdose on than alcohol. You can have too much of anything for your own good. But weed wasn't taking our family members, or destroying our community. Crack was.

And at the time, weed was almost as illegal as crack. Which meant you could make almost as much money selling it.

Without legal businesses selling weed, anyone who was willing to risk arrest could tap into a market that was used to paying premium prices. Because the business was illegal, there were no taxes or regulations on it. And you could grow weed in almost any climate.

Even in a basement. Selling weed was as simple as finding somebody who grew it, buying from them, and selling at a markup to local users and hustlers.

The big suppliers we found were mostly rich, white, dudes who lived in mansions surrounded by so much farmland or forest that no one cared what went on there. California, Tennessee, Colorado, Alabama, Georgia, and West Virginia all grew unbelievable amounts of weed. It was one of their major exports.

I found my connects through people I knew in the business. Harold and Ray were thirty-something, inheritors of their parents' land and money, educated at Ivy Leagues. They also loved to party more than anything. Drugs had been an essential part of having a good time for them since high school, and as far as they were concerned they were just sharing the wealth.

Selling weed was the easiest money imaginable for them. Marijuana got its nickname because it literally *is* a weed. It's actually harder to stop it from growing than to make it grow. All they had to do was scatter seeds, wait a few months, and harvest. In their spare time they experimented with cross-breeding strains and improving the quality of their crop, but they hardly had to work it like a full-time job. And it paid much better than anything legal.

Harold and Ray had been supplying Maryland and Washington, D.C. for years. They liked to fly out in their private jet and snort crushed-up pills and coke at parties with their big money customers once in a while.

Jordan and I were two of those customers. We didn't touch the pills or the coke, but we drank and laughed along with them while they bragged about the fancy trips they were taking their girls on with all this this weed money.

A pound of weed could be bought for about $500, and sold for over $1,000. Shipments from Harold and Ray came in the hundreds of pounds. They'd have them flown out by private jet, and it would be picked up at the airport. Drivers were paid to deliver.

Our one rule was never broken: never bring any of the stuff home. Get it from the airport and then immediately unloaded it to clients and distributors in the nearby cities.

Getting caught with 100 pounds of weed in your garage meant kingpin charges. A mandatory minimum of twenty years in prison.

In the weed business, customers were mostly white. Serving D. C. and Baltimore meant serving the rich kids and the poor kids alike. Black customers from the hood were more likely to order smaller amounts - anywhere from half an ounce to ¼ of a pound, which was usually the most hood customers could afford out-of-pocket. White kids or businessmen from uptown, on the other hand, might order whole pounds at a time, shelling out hundreds or thousands of dollars to supply their friends at parties.

We liked to party too - though we never touched the stuff we sold. We'd seen what that could do to people. Instead it was all high-end liquor, good food, and good music.

A few months into the operation, Jordan and I bought a house in a good neighborhood that had two different hot tubs. One for each of us. We decorated most of the rooms with big screen TVs, got the best furniture and the best art. Ours was gonna be a classy place, we'd decided. A place where kids from the hood could come to feel like they were part of something important.

We also poured money into cars. At one point I bought a luxury Infiniti - already a powerful car - and then spent $15,000 souping up the engine and customizing the look. Cars were status symbols, and mine screamed 'success.'

We took our friends and family out to clubs, to restaurants. When me and Jordan were entertaining, the food and drinks were all on us. We even took our homies on trips to tropical paradises.

It wasn't all fun and fast cars. When we weren't partying we were helping friends and family with bills, mortgages, school tuition, and anything else they might need. When little old ladies or kids back in the hood got in trouble, we were there for them. We felt especially good about doing that without selling crack. In our hands, we reasoned, weed was a form of wealth redistribution. The stuff didn't destroy lives the way crack did, and the money came mostly from rich folks and flowed through us into the hoods we came from.

The money was so good and the risk to our own community so small that soon, we forgot all about our plans to make a legit business. It seemed like we could keep money flowing to ourselves and our friends and family forever, even without selling other drugs.

But the high life never lasts.

It started with a fight. I was at a baseball game in our nice, new neighborhood, with a beautiful woman at my side. Like always, I was treating my girl to the best of everything. We brought hot dogs and buns and beer for the adults. We were chillin' in lawn chairs, having a good time, watching the local kids play while their parents cheered them on.

But then a dude decided to mess with my woman.

"Hey, how much for a spin?" he asked, clearly referring to

her body.

Where I come from, showin' off your assets is just what people do. Just 'cause a woman is showin' off her beauty doesn't mean she's tryin' to sell it to you, any more than me shown off my custom Infiniti means I'm tryin' to sell you *that*.

I stood up, striking an aggressive front. "What is your problem?!"

My childhood training kicked in fast.

I don't remember what he said. I don't remember what *I* said. All I remember is that, at some point, he shoved me. It was more of a light tap, really. A symbolic gesture.

My vision went red.

On the street, you don't tolerate disrespect. On the street, it can be fatal. In a world where nobody's got anything and you defend what you've got with guns, you show folks that they don't mess with you or else you'll mess with them. Doing that, mostly, keeps people off your ass. If you make yourself a high-cost target, they will avoid you if they can help it.

Street logic doesn't work in the suburbs.

When I came out of my rage, the dude was on the ground in front of me. Like he was a kid in a backyard fighting ring. The conditioning never left me. If somebody hits you, you hit them back *hard*. Make them never want to hit you again.

But my fists were still moving against my will.. Slamming again and again into this dude's face. I looked down at him and knew that it was over, that I'd already gone too far, that I didn't need to keep going. But I guess my fists didn't get the message.

I must have looked like I got some control back then, because two dudes came in and pulled me off of him. I didn't fight them. At least, not very much.

The dude on the ground didn't position to move. He was lying in a pool of blood. Nearby, my woman was looking at me, horrified. So were a whole bunch of moms and dads and kids.

"Shit," I said.

The guys who pulled me off were only too glad to get rid of me. I shook them off, walked backward from the circle of judging stares in a daze.

Man. I really fucked up.

As much as I wanted to live in a world where people didn't beat each other up for money or respect, some part of me still lived in a world where they did. Some part of me still thought that's what it takes to survive.

I started walking home. Walking like leaving the scene of a crime. Like any scene in the hood, I expected I could leave it behind me by walking away. Back home somebody would hit you back, or they wouldn't. No in between, no third option.

Back in the hood, nobody called the cops.

☆☆☆

The cops came two days later. At the worst possible time.

A shipment of a couple hundred pounds of weed arrived, and there was about twenty pounds of it left to unload. It arrived in the trunk of the car, out to a spot in town where a client was supposed to come pick it up.

Problem was, the dude didn't arrive.

We waited and waited. Darkness fell around the car. Three hours after the hand-off was supposed to take place, my phone battery died. There was no car charger, .. no way of reaching the buyer,, and nowhere safe to put $20,000 worth of raw product.

Reluctantly, figuring one time should be fine, Jordan and I drove home to our mansion in the burbs. The weed sat in the car overnight, in the garage, for somebody else to hand it off to in the morning.

☆☆☆

Bang bang bang. Someone was pounding on our front door.

I dragged myself out of bed, threw on my Versace robe, and skidded into the hall. Outside, it was still dark. I glanced at one of the gold clocks we had hanging on the wall. 5am. I stood still, waiting for some action.

Cops. There were cops outside the door.

"Good morning, officer," I said, opening the door and squinting.

"Hawk?" He didn't wait for me to answer. "We have a warrant for your arrest for an assault occurring last Saturday."

"Ah, shit," I said.

But I wasn't too worried. Jordan and I could afford the best lawyers. I knew from talking to the rich plugs I'd bought from and sold to that being able to afford the best lawyers meant you could get away with *anything.*

"Alright officer, I'll come with you." I stepped out of the front door and closed it behind me, eager to hide the big-screen TVs and leather furniture that decorated the living room from the officers' view.

The cops looked me up and down and laughed. "Boy, are you wearing anything under that robe? We can't take you in like that. Go put some pants on."

I hesitated.

That was a mistake. As I hesitated, one of the officers grabbed my arm and started to pull me back into the house. Another reached for my front door and threw it open. The first officer pulled me too hard and I tripped on the step, cracking my head on the marble floor of the entryway as I fell.

"Bruh! Are you okay?"

Jordan came scrambling around the corner from the hall where the bedrooms were, a joint hanging from his lips.

"They've got drugs!" The officer who had my other arm yelled. The second officer rushed Jordan and tackled him, pinning him to the ground. He was wearing a Versace robe too, nothing underneath. But the officer still frisked him assuming he had a gun somewhere.

"You can't search the house without a warrant!" I knew that much from the time I spent studying Law Enforcement and Criminal Justice. I knew every regulation these guys were *supposed* to follow. But I don't know why I expected that to matter.

The cops started tearing the place apart. I don't know if they found the stuff in the trunk before or after they started trying on our watches and shoes and ripping holes in the wall looking for cash. I didn't dare get up off the ground with two armed officers running around my crib like little kids on Christmas morning, so I wasn't in a position to know.

I knew they'd gone *bad* off the books when the off-duty officers showed up. About twelve guys who moved like they had police training rolled up in a van, out of uniform, and they took everything.

Everything. Our shoes, clothes, and jewelry. The big-screen TVs from every room, the radios and the huge speakers from the living room. They found every bag of cash. The ones under the bed and the ones in the closets, the ones in the safe that they just *took* lifted and put into their van without bothering to crack it.

Jordan and I watched from the floor in disbelief as the cops tore our house apart. Compared to the treatment from cops I was used to dealing with in the hood, this was *beyond* illegal.

Finally, the house had been gutted. Furniture and walls lay broken, and every valuable that could be moved was in the back of that van. The cops found enough drugs to put us behind bars on a high cash bail - that we wouldn't be able to pay, because they had our cash and they'd freeze our bank accounts on suspicion of drug money.

When there was nothing left to take, the two guys who showed up in the first place put us in their car and drove us downtown. The other twelve dudes drove their van full of our stuff in the opposite direction, going who-knows where.

Jordan and I didn't speak as the cops drove us down to the precinct. In my head, wheels were turning a mile a minute.

Were we gonna end up like the guys I'd seen in Maryland State Prison, serving twenty years to life for possession? Would I be sitting in a cell twenty-three hours a day, getting let out once a day to exercise in the prison courtyard?

I didn't really think it was going to come to that, because the way they'd 'searched' our house was so blatantly illegal. 'Looting' was a better word for it. I didn't expect to arrive at the precinct to find that they had come back to report all our cash and big screen TVs and put them in an evidence locker. No, the cops who did it were long gone and clearly expected to get away with it.

They probably also didn't know I was a former correctional officer with a degree in Law Enforcement and Criminal Justice.

Jordan and I sat in the local jail's holding cells for two days. Our cash was gone and our bank accounts were frozen. We could have called friends and family for help making bail so we could get out before our court date. But Jordan and I had always done things a little differently from most hustlers. When things went wrong, we stopped to think.

Making bail would only be a temporary solution to our problems. We needed lawyers - good ones. How were we going to pay for them? Some of our friends might have had the money to put up. But before we asked anyone for anything, we had to take stock of what we had, and make sure we had a solid case.

When the station's detectives took us aside to interrogate us about the drugs, it was obvious that they didn't know anything about what the dirty cops had taken. Most important, they hadn't turned in our bags of cash. If they had, the precinct would have hit us with kingpin charges. Having lots of cash on the same premises of drugs was considered proof of distribution.

And all the missing evidence meant we had an ace up our sleeves.

I didn't say anything except: "I want to talk to my lawyer." I said that two or three times.

Now that we knew what the precinct had, it was time to call for help. A few of our friends got together the money to hire good lawyers - the rich person's remedy to all problems - and we told those lawyers what we knew.

I remember my lawyer's eyes getting real big when I told him the story of the day we were arrested. "They took the televisions, the speakers - even your clothes?"

"Yes, sir."

"And there's...evidence of this?"

"Well, there's an empty house with lots of holes in the wall, broken furniture, and a bunch of stands where TVs and speakers used to be. And no cash or anything else reported on the precinct books. If that ain't evidence of robbery, I don't know what is!"

Our lawyer put through a request to the detectives' office, to examine our house to verify my story. When the detectives' story didn't match up, we dropped our bombshell:

"The twelve men who took your things - are you certain they were officers?"

"Well whoever they were, they sure as hell knew the dudes in uniform. The guys with the van and the uniformed officers went through the house together, and the officers sure didn't try to stop them. In fact, I don't know who else could have called them - me and my brother were on the ground." I glanced at Jordan.

"Did you happen to get the license plate of this van?"

"Yeah," I said, "I did."

☆☆☆

I don't know what happened with the dirty cops. Maybe they weren't even off-duty police - who knows. But as for 'how much' evidence we had against them, the answer was 'too much.'

The State's Attorney only prosecuted us for possession and asked for eighteen months' probation - on the condition that we didn't take our story to the press. As deals with the devil go, this was a damn good one. Our silence in exchange for our lives.

I had a lot of time to think while I was staring at the ceiling at night, wondering if we'd spend the best years of our lives behind bars.

I thought about the hustlers I'd known, almost all of them dead or incarcerated by forty.

I thought about all the dudes in Maryland State Prison - ninety percent of them looking like me, most behind bars for petty crimes or nonviolent drug offenses.

I thought about all the rich white dudes that *weren't* - the ones the cops wouldn't touch – who held an advantage that we just didn't have.

It was time to get out of the game for real.

The day after the judge's decision came. We'd been spared. No prison time, no life sentence. We had to rebuild from nothing - no cash, a house in massive need of repairs. Jordan and I went our separate ways to get our heads together for a few days. We had to figure out a *legal* way to make ends meet.

Then one day, I got a call from him.

"Hey Hawk," he said, "how do you feel about selling shoes?"

HEAVY

I been lost myself now I'm going insane,
I been stressing - fuck y'all judging me,
None of y'all motherfuckers care for me,
Y'all wasn't there for me
Fuck, y'all think y'all family?

It was a hot summer day when I got the call from Charles. My sister was in the hospital.

Delilah was a few years younger than me. She was in her late teens now, and suffering from the consequences of our childhood. Trauma loves misery. She'd been born to Charles and Nolita the first year after they got together. Charles and I had protected her as best we could, but Nolita's addiction touched everything. Delilah had stayed with my mother while I went out hustling and Charles went to work. She'd stayed with us in the rat-infested, candlelit house after my mother kicked Charles out, until foster care came to get her. God only knows what my mother did to her, given what she did to me.

Now, Delilah was in the hospital. In a psychiatric hospital, to be exact. Charles had convinced her to check herself in after finding her taking a razor blade to her arms. When he confronted her, she told him she wanted to die.

Delilah wanted to see our mother. And Charles knew I was the one who could always find Nolita.

I hated what was happening to Delilah. I hated that my mother could have done that to her. We all knew it was my mother's neglect and the things she had exposed Delilah to that lead to this. Delilah couldn't have been much safer with our mother than our mother was with Mary.

Anxiety was like acid in my blood as I drove my pearl-white Infiniti G37 with HAWK custom-painted on the windshield up to the house where Nolita was living with her new husband, Heavy.

It was a crack house, essentially - not quite an abandominium, but a broken-down old place where Heavy sold vials and my mother and his other customers used them, and he turned just about enough profit to keep the lights on. I'd never liked Heavy, but I had to feel sorry for him. Like my mother, he was an example of dreams broken by addiction.

Once upon a time, Heavy had been an OG. He'd been a high-roller, respected and known. Like so many OGs, he was a benefactor. Paying people's mortgages, tuition, and supporting the neighborhood out of the massive amounts of drug money he brought in.

But Heavy made the worst mistake a hustler can make: he tried what he was selling.

Hustlers know what drugs do to people. Their business model depends on people selling their very lives to get more money to give to the hustlers. That's why none of them use - not if they want to make it to the top.

Within a few months of starting to smoke the crack himself, Heavy's business tanked. He was missing deadlines, not showing up for deals, making sloppy mistakes. His temper got erratic, too. That's something you really can't afford in a business that involves hundreds of thousands in cash, lots of guns, and people shooting at you.

Heavy made out better than a lot of fiends - he stayed functional enough to be able to hustle on a corner, make a living wage, have some vestiges of respect from when he used to be an OG. But all the other OGs knew he was compromised - unreliable, not strategic. He'd lost all the things you would want in a business partner or benefactor. With coke-clouded vision, he'd never be a mover or shaker. He'd be lucky to live past fifty.

Now, he was just a spent old man - old for that neighborhood - a cautionary tale, a reminder to all the young hustlers to never use what you sell. He was doing at forty what most hustlers were doing in their teens, and he was stuck there.

As I rolled up to Heavy's house, I saw my mother sitting on the doorstep. She was talking to Heavy. It was hard to believe it was my mother: her curves, her glow, and her smile were gone. She was skinny, messy, and twice Aunt Patty's age. I tried to imagine Aunt Patty being ten years older than the woman in front of me.

As I'd hoped, my mother looked up, saw my car, and recognized it as mine. But her response hurt. Her eyes got real big and and she ran inside the crack house. Hiding from me just like she used to hide from Charles.

It was rage that boiled in me then, white hot. What kind of mother runs away when she sees her child coming?!

I was already close to the edge when I got out of the car, slamming the door behind me, too hard. Heavy was still standing by the door of the house, looking at me, playing it cool.

"Hey hey Shorty, what brings you to town?"

"I need to see my mother. You're gonna have to get her for me."

Heavy smiled, playing for time. "What's your rush, man?"

I put my foot down - literally stomped my foot, my new Nikes crunching on the gravelly sidewalk. "My sister's in the hospital. She wants her mother. Go get her."

Heavy looked around, uneasy. I could see he wasn't any more thrilled than I was about trying to make Nolita do something she didn't want to do.

At that moment, two young dudes strolled up to Heavy's stoop. It was clear from the way they moved that they knew Heavy, and were here for a transaction. He pulled a prescription pill bottle out of his pocket before they even asked. Ignoring me, he opened the container, poured out maybe a dozen little white discs, and counted them.

Something in me snapped. I slapped Heavy's hand, scattering the pills on the ground. "*Go get my mother.*" I demanded, my voice rising.

"Hey!" the young dudes yelled, angry. "Those were our pills! You've gotta pay for them!"

I stomped on the sidewalk, crushing little white discs beneath my feet.

"The hell are you doing?!" Heavy yelled, looking at his ruined merchandise.

One of the young dudes swung at me. My vision went red.

In less than a minute the young dudes and I were punching each other, Heavy was punching me for interfering with his business, and I was ping-ponging between the three of them, landing blows and dodging but still getting bloodied up myself. I was back in the basement fighting rings, back with my mother. I may have been outnumbered, but Heavy was old and the other two dudes were inexperienced.

Never let them see you weak.

God only knows how the fight would have ended if the local OG hadn't come rolling down the block. He stopped the car and jumped out, alarmed.

"Heavy, man! What the fuck! You gonna make the block hot!"

That was enough to stop all of us. *Nobody* wanted the cops coming out and deciding we'd become dangerous.

The OG came around his car, all blinged-out and clean. His frown deepened as he saw me.

"Hawk? Shorty? Heavy, why the fuck you beating up Nolita's boy?"

"He trashed my pills!" Heavy protested.

"*Our* pills," one of the other dudes said.

The OG held his hand up. "I've known Shorty since he was little. He don't do nothing without a good reason. So you gonna tell me Shorty? Why you up here making our block hot?"

I was wiping blood from my eyes, along with tears of frustration. "My mother's inside," my voice cracked. "My little sister's in the hospital, and she's asking to see her mother. My ma won't come out."

The OG's frown got deeper still. He turned to Heavy. "Go get Nono."

"But - " Heavy protested, "this kid's the one that came out here and started fucking up my business. You gonna let that go?"

"Shorty's tryin' to save his family. He gets respect. I don't want him down here anymore than you do, but I ain't gonna mess him up for tryin' to save his mother and his sister. Go get Nono. You know he ain't gonna leave without her, and if he stays he *will* make the block hot."

Heavy retreated, grumbling and dripping blood. The two young dudes stood aside, clearly out of their depth.

I stood there, shaking, trying to get ahold of myself. This wasn't what I'd planned when I came to get my mother. This wasn't what I'd planned at all.

Heavy came out of the house a few minutes later with another dude, Nolita between them. She wasn't exactly struggling, but they were herding her like some kind of stubborn animal that didn't want to move. I watched as Heavy opened my passenger side door and the two dudes put my mother in my car. She just kind of sat there in the car, looking at the shiny leather interior blankly.

"Yo, thanks man," I said to the OG. My feelings were sincere. If he hadn't decided to help me, the situation could have been a lot worse - even dangerous.

The OG nodded, looking at the ground. "You always had a good heart, Shorty," he said. "What goes on with your mother - it's a shame, you know? It ain't Heavy's fault - ain't nobody who can stop Nono when she sets her mind to a thing. But we'd fix her up if we could."

I nodded, touched. It's the open secret of the hustler, the contradiction of it: you need other people to be using, but you don't want it to be anybody who you like or love.

I got in the car and drove away.

Sitting in the driver's seat beside my mother was surreal. Since leaving Aunt Patty's, my only real contact with her had been visits I made to talk with her, to try to understand what she was doing. Aunt Patty had encouraged me to do that - to see what good I could salvage from my mother, after she took what could have been my adoptive home from me.

Now, in the silence of my sports car, my mother didn't say anything to me.

"Ma," I said finally, as the street passed outside in a blur, "Delilah's sick."

She looked at me sidelong. "What's that got to do with me?"

"She wants to see you."

"Oh."

My mother stared ahead. Didn't seem to know what to do

with that information.

"Ma - " I tried.

"Do you have fifty dollars?"

I turned and stared at her, forgetting for a minute about the road.

"I just need - I need a hit, real quick, before we go see her. I can't be in withdrawal when I see my daughter."

"Ma, I'm *not* getting you drugs so you can be high while you talk to my sister!"

"Just a fifty, Hawk. Please."

She turned and looked at me then with this awful, pleading gaze. I was confused as much as anything. We'd just left the crack house where she was married to the hustler. How bad could her need be?

"No, Ma! I am bringing you to see Delilah, and you're gonna be sober while you do it!"

My mother looked around. Looked at the shiny leather armrest, the spotless clean back seat. Looked at my pocket. Looking for my wallet, I realized.

"It'll just be a few hours," I told her. "If you can just hold it together for *a few hours* - "

The passenger door opened, and I swerved. I think I screamed. My mother threw herself out of the moving car, hitting the pavement at a roll. I pulled over on the shoulder of the road so fast my wheels screeched, but she was already picking herself up and walking away from me. I watched her in my rearview mirror.

That was when I lost it.

I was that little boy all over again, my mother putting me in the fighting ring and telling me I'd better not lose. I was sitting at Aunt Patty's kitchen table, telling the social worker that Phillip hit me because my mother told me to. I knew I'd be sitting in a hospital room with my sister, cuts all over her arms, telling her that her mother wasn't coming to see her because she'd rather be smoking crack.

I sat there on the side of the road and cried, sobs tearing out of me like a poison leaving my system. I cried for two hours.

When I came back to myself, it was getting dark. Cars with headlights on were whizzing by.

My sister was waiting for me.

In two hours, nobody had stopped to see what was up with a black man in a fancy car, stopped by the side of the road and hunched over his steering wheel. I knew that was for the best - a cop would've taken one look at my car, the color of my skin, and the blood on my clothes and tried to book me for something.

I wiped the blood out of my eyes, sat up, and drove.

At the hospital, the charge nurse's eyes got big when she saw me. One of my eyes was swollen shut and a bruise was swelling on the side of my face. There was enough blood on my shirt to be alarming, and I didn't feel like explaining that most of it came from Heavy and the other two dudes who fought me over the cost of their pills.

"I'm here to see my sister," I said, my speech a little slurred from the bruises. A couple of other nurses came up and tried to get me to sit down, started trying to check me in as a patient.

"No, I'm fine. I'm not a patient. I'm here to see my sister."

A couple of the nurses recognized me, had seen me here earlier promising Delilah I would bring our mom back with me. They silently escorted me to her room, where Delilah lay under a sterile hospital blanket, looking into space with a dead stare.

Charles sat in a chair by the hospital room door with his head bowed. He looked up when I came in, and I saw by his face that he instantly knew what had happened. The blood. The bruises. The fact that I was alone.

I sat down in the empty chair beside him, and for a long minute nobody said anything.

"She ain't coming, is she?" Delilah asked, not looking at me.

I didn't say anything.

"Hawk," Charles said finally, "I'm sorry Nono didn't come. I mean it. But I'm not surprised. You wanna survive, you've got to stop chasing your mother." He looked at Delilah. "You both do."

"I've been through everything you're going through now. When she kicked me out, it was 'cause we both knew I was gonna get myself killed, or get somebody else killed, if I kept chasing her. If I kept trying to save her. I know you love her, 'cause I love her too. But you've gotta let her go."

I sat in that hospital chair and looked at my sister.

We were family. Three people connected by Nolita. Nolita wasn't here with us, and she never would be. But we were here for each other.

I realized right then that we always would be family.

WITH HONOR

Whatcha know bout the young poor stuck in a hole?
Running thru them streets where it's always cold
Young boys hustling, guns steady busting,
Females tricking, selling their gold

I knew now that I couldn't keep hustling. But I had to do something with my brain. And I had a pretty good idea what that was.

There was a whole field of study devoted to criminal justice. I already knew what the laws were, and why. But how did you change them? That went beyond an Associate's Degree level. That was what all those future lawyers and politicians were studying up at the universities.

So I applied to college using my Associate's Degree credentials, and got admitted to the University of Baltimore's Criminal Justice Bachelor's Degree program.

Nestled into an upscale part of Baltimore, its campus was dominated by tall brick buildings filled with classrooms and lecture halls. Peppered around them were dozens of little restaurants and cafes where students studied and talked. Some nearby historic houses had become student residences, so that a whole section of the city was owned or rented by the University and its students.

My first day on campus was jarring. Why? All the white people, and how it felt to be alone in a room with them.

In my schools, my neighborhood, at Maryland State - in all of them, I'd been surrounded mostly by black people. I knew white people, of course - but I always saw them in mixed environments. I'd never gone to white schools or white churches where I was the only different person there.

So I was surprised by how hard it hit me. Hard. Even to a guy who'd fought with a hustler and two fiends not so long ago, being suddenly surrounded by people who didn't look like, talk like me, move like me, was *scary*.

I'd expected to find the University's campus to be beautiful. I hadn't expected that almost none of the people there would be like me.

There were other black people at the University, of course. There were about five of them in that first lecture hall. There were also Asian, Hispanic, and Middle Eastern folks. But it seemed white people made up 90% of the student body, easy. They talked differently, moved differently, even seemed to see the world differently than I was used to. And that felt profoundly weird.

It felt like I was somewhere I wasn't supposed to be.

No one was mean to me - at least, not at first. I think they really tried to make me feel comfortable. But nothing quite takes away the feeling that you are somewhere that isn't made for you when you can look around and not see anybody who looks like you or talks like you nearby.

I wasn't about to let that stop me. Not even a little. If anything, it made me more determined. I'd always been the sort of person to hear 'you can't do that' and take it as a challenge.

But it was surprising. It was a challenge I hadn't expected.

It wasn't just the color of my skin - the culture was different too, in ways I couldn't quite define. Often I'd see my classmates meeting each other - daughters and sons of doctors and lawyers - and see them sizing each other up for things I didn't understand. I knew what sizing somebody up looked like - I think that is essential to every culture. But they sure weren't sizing each other up for new shoes, gold chains, or the kind of swagger you get from winning every fight you've ever been in.

So what were they looking for? Probably something I didn't have.

Well. I had more important things to worry about.

I slowly realized this school would be real different from my Associates' Degree. That program had been meant for cops, prison guards, and other people whose main job was following orders, following the law.

This program was meant for people who meant to change the law. It was meant for future lawyers, and future politicians. At the University, we weren't just going to be taught what law and law enforcement *were*. We were going to be taught how to question them. And by 'we,' I mean 'myself, and an entire room of people who only knew what television told them about crime.'

The most difficult class was also one of my first. It was a statistics class - but it wasn't the math that tripped me up. Instead, it was the open discussions. It was the things people said in them.

And the things they didn't say.

The class talked about statistics like racial representation in the prison system. Arrest rates vs. actual crime rates. Crime rates among different races. One week, our reading revealed that black men were drastically overrepresented in the prison system. The majority of all men in prison in the United States were black. Only 13% of American men *out* of prison were black.

"Well I mean, that makes sense, doesn't it?" one girl in the front row asked. "I mean there is a *lot* of crime in black communities, isn't there?"

In the back row, my hand shot up. I think everybody around me sensed that she'd stepped in something, but they didn't realize it wasn't just indignation about stereotyping.

I was pissed, but not at her. I was pissed that none of the realities I had seen were in the textbooks the school was giving these kids.

"Hawk," the teacher called on me.

"Well," I said to her, "you're right. There is a lot of crime in black communities. I know because I came from one. But there's also a lot of crime in *white* communities that isn't on the books. The cops pick who to arrest. And they don't pick you."

It was time for me to lay my cards on the table. Otherwise, they'd never believe me.

"I used to sell drugs," I told the class. "And I saw a lot of stuff in the streets that isn't anywhere in these books. Yeah, a lot of people in my hood was using and selling drugs. But we also had white customers. Hell, we had white *suppliers*. A lot of the hustlers in the hood got their raw materials from rich white dudes. Did y'all know yet can get punished the same for a handful of crack as a whole briefcase full of powdered coke?"

My classmates were staring at me, wide-eyed. I wondered if I'd just fucked up my academic career. But I kept going. I couldn't stop.

"When I worked in Maryland State as a correctional officer, the folks there were 90% black. Where were the rich dudes we bought bricks from? Where were the white folks who came to the hood specifically to buy crack from us? Where were the white college kids I sold bags of vials to so they could sell them on campus? They weren't in the prison. Only the poor black dudes were."

I looked around. "Y'all guys gotta *know* this stuff if you're gonna be lawyers or make a change at all," I finished.

For a moment, there was heavy silence.

At the front of the classroom, the professor, slowly, started to applaud.

☆☆☆

That set the tone for the rest of the semester. We'd read some bullshit in our books that failed to report all the arrests that weren't made, all the crimes that weren't reported, all the reasons *why* people in the hood became hustlers or got hooked on drugs. I'd do my best to add the missing information.

The professor supported me. But it got to be draining, constantly going up against a huge tide of people who had never seen anything you saw and who probably suspected, somewhere in their brains, that you were lying.

Some students wanted to be friends. That class was where I met Angelina, a brown-eyed, white 18-year-old with supermodel looks who was on the path to become a lawyer like her daddy. She was the kind of person who seemed like she didn't belong in the same world as me, but she respected me. She asked the right questions. She seemed to care.

The difference between her world and the one I grew up in was brought home in an unexpected way: by campus parties.

Despite my background - or maybe because of it - I got popular pretty fast. If nothing else, I had 'street cred,' which was something that even the rich sons of lawyers wanted to pretend they had, even as they argued for locking up my people for having it.

I got invited to all the best parties. And here, 'best' meant 'craziest.'

I'd been introduced to the world of crazy white kids' parties through Jordan's high school classmates. These kids - also children of doctors, lawyers, judges, etc., - got hold of drugs we'd never even *heard* of on the street. They'd show me pills and I'd be like 'what is this?'

Using opioids wasn't a thing in the hood in my day - mostly because doctors wouldn't prescribe them to us - and other drugs like shrooms and LSD were seen as an exotic waste of time. Why use hallucinogens when you had a high you knew you could trust? Why spend a lot of time procuring something from some fancy gardner or chemist when you could buy crack on every corner?

The kids at Jordan's school had everything that bored, rich kids could get hold of and show off to their friends. I saw some crazy behavior at those parties that I still don't understand.

University parties, it turned out, were just like that. But they looked different to me now, after what I'd seen and been through.

I got invited to the first one by Angelina - with the support of her boyfriend, Brad, who thought that having me around would make him look cool. I drove up in my pearl-white Infiniti, so bright it even kind of hurt your eyes at night, and parked it among all the other rich kids' cars. As I got out of the car, music was pounding through the walls and windows of the frat house.

"Hey, it's Hawk," some dude from my statistics class called, waving. I didn't know his name because he never talked, but he obviously knew mine. I waved at him and sauntered inside, pretending I owned the place.

In reality, I had no idea what to expect. I'd been to college parties at Morgan when I worked there, and to high school parties with Jordan's private school friends. But Morgan is a historically black college, and it wasn't full of white people with a family tradition of wealth. I wondered how the white lawyers of tomorrow partied.

I found out real quick.

Inside, the music that was pounding turned out to be hip hop. Somebody had gotten a bunch of colored light bulbs from somewhere, so everything was dim and blue and green and purple. People weren't packed as tightly as some parties I'd been to - but there was a reason for that.

The front room was empty because everybody was in the back room - where the party was. Away from the windows and prying eyes of neighbors, a few of the University's finest women had pulled their shirts up and were assisting some of its finest men in snorting lines of cocaine off of their bare breasts.

One of the women looked at me. "Oh, hey Hawk!" She also recognized me from class. I recognized her as 'blonde chick who sits in the corner.'

"Hey."

By the way she was looking at me, I could tell she was expecting me to get in line to do drugs off her body, but I just kinda stood back awkwardly. She was looking at me like that was some sort of standard *greeting* around here, like I'd be rude if I *didn't*, but if there's one thing you learn as a hustler it's that you *never* touch the stuff you sell.

Also, I'd never snorted coke off someone as a greeting before.

One of the frat boys who was hosting the thing came up to me, put his arm around my shoulder like we were friends. Like we were homies. Like we'd struggled together, relied on each other. Like I could rely on him.

Thinking real hard about why he looked familiar, I remembered him sitting in the front row of one of my classes. I remembered that one time I'd overheard him talking about flirting with a female teaching assistant to try to get better grades.

"Hey man, hey," he said. "I was wondering, Hawk, you know - you still in the business?"

What 'business' he meant was pretty obvious. "No," I said, stone-faced.

He looked at me real close, his blue eyes studying mine. "You know if you are, you can tell me." He gestured around. "It's not like I'm gonna call the cops."

"I got out of that business, yo," I told him. "I'm not lookin' to get anybody else addicted."

"Come *on* Hawk," he said. "Powder isn't anywhere near as addictive as crack. You know that. It isn't dangerous. Just a little off your next shipment? I can pay better than anybody."

For some bizarre reason, at that point I started laughing. I laughed so hard and so loud that the kid - whatever his name was - let go of me and moved away, tried to look casual. I guess he figured I was laughing at him.

"Man," I managed, wiping the tears from my eyes, "y'all do what you're gonna do. But I ain't selling no more. Not now. Not ever."

Truth was, I knew some corpses who would disagree with him about powdered coke not being dangerous or addictive. But I wasn't about to go lecturing these kids about dangerous behavior after the stories I'd told them in class.

And sometimes, when something hurts, you've just gotta laugh about it.

☆☆☆

I don't need to tell you that getting at that degree wasn't easy. I didn't learn to read and write *at all* until I was ten, and graduated high school reading well below grade level. It was hard work for me. Harder than it was, probably, for any of the other students.

But I was motivated as *hell*. These were my people's lives we were talking about in these classes. I'd been there - on the inside, on the outside, and now at the top where people didn't even know about me and mine. Something had to change.

So I was gonna change it.

I caught on pretty fast to the idea that my classmates didn't expect me to do well. I may have had the street smarts, they thought, but I had to be lacking in other areas. No way a hustler from the hood was as smart as them.

I was determined to prove them wrong, and to do it in the most spectacular way possible.

For those years I ate, slept, and breathed books. The property management business didn't require much of my attention, and everything else took a back seat.

Sometimes I had to grit my teeth.

Once, one of the lawyers of the future actually showed up to an exam high on ecstacy. I know it was ecstacy, because he told the kids behind him in a stage whisper. It was an exam about drug sentencing laws.

Another time, I heard a kid whose parents were both doctors whining that they 'made him' take an expensive college prep program last summer. I thought about how many hood kids would have *killed* for that opportunity, if they'd even thought that college and professional careers were realistic enough to apply for.

I was gonna show 'em. I was gonna show those hood kids, and these rich kids both that somebody like me could roll with the best of 'em from the good neighborhoods.

I wasn't just going to graduate. I was going to do it with honors.

There were good people too, among those rich kids. Good friends. Angelina became embarrassed of her frat boy boyfriend and eventually broke up with him. She and some other especially ambitious students would study with me in the library, long after classes were over.

Much of the world might have run on parties and drugs, but we weren't interested in escaping. We realized what drugs were - an escape that leaves everybody else behind.

Instead of escaping the world, we were gonna change it.

☆☆☆

I couldn't sleep the night before my graduation. I was too excited.

I paced around my house, half dancing, trying to tire myself out. When that didn't work, I lay in bed, fidgeting like a little kid the night before Christmas.

I fantasized about graduation day. Proof that I could do what they said I couldn't. Getting my degree from a fancy white University. Neither my parents nor any of their kids had even gone to college. Any college. Much less a fancy state university. Much less *graduated* from such a university.

I figured it would be the crowning achievement of my life. It would also be my gateway to real success, to changing the course of life for generations after me. Aunt Patty-style success.

I lay awake remembering classrooms where it was forty kids and one teacher, no real learning going on. I remembered concluding there was no reason to be there, like most hood kids eventually did.

I remembered struggling to read, being so ashamed that I *couldn't*. That everything that went on in the schools in Aunt Patty's good district with their good property taxes was like Greek or Latin to me. Remembered feeling more powerless than I'd felt in a long time, like there was a whole world I was shut out of.

I remembered coasting through high school, putting in my dues so I could get basic employment but thinking, the way guys from the hood always did, that college wasn't for me. Nobody I knew had succeeded on that path. The people who were successful, who made it rain for their friends and families and communities, were the hustlers.

But now I'd been through every ringer life had to throw at me - poverty, illiteracy, physical danger, criminal charges, boring jobs. And I'd found out college was right for me. It was the only way for me to do what I wanted to do.

And I'd done it. With a GPA of 3.6, I was set to graduate *cum laude* - a Latin phrase meaning 'with honor.' That meant I was one of the highest-performing students in my graduating class. I'd done it. In spite of everything.

I jumped out of bed way too early in the morning and started dancing around in my underwear, calling everybody I knew to make sure they'd be there on time.

Karlie was coming to the ceremony, and so was my biological dad. And my brother, Jordan, the private school prince who'd supported me every step of the way. Members of our crew - just because you stopped the hustle didn't mean you lost that hard-earned camaraderie of homies.

I threw on my fancy shirt and pants, smiling with the thought that they'd be hidden under my graduation robe, and took off for the stadium where commencement would be.

When I got there, I was in a sea of identical robes and caps.

Well, almost identical. *Cum laude* students wore an extra gold cord, like a fancy rope with a tassel, draped around our necks against the black of our robes.

It was totally crazy to be up there with all those lawyers and criminal investigators of the future. Never in a million years would my teenage self have seen my future self here.

I found a spot near Angelina, and we gathered to wait for the speeches to start.

Every college graduation has a whole slew of speeches. These graduates going out into the world are a big deal, and everybody wants a piece of it. The President of the University talks about how great and inspiring the class has been. Then the Student Body President says the same thing about their classmates. At first it feels amazing to be one of those graduates they're bragging about, but eventually you start to fidget, like *'Give us our degrees already!'*

Finally walking up to that stage and getting that degree in my hand felt surreal. It was a moment I'd never thought I'd have. A moment that had seemed like it was for other people, when I was younger. I think I held the piece of paper up and pumped my fist a little.

The crowd went wild, and I knew the loudest cheers were coming from my homies.

When the formal ceremony was over, it was time to mingle. Students and family members flooded out of the stands, forming a huge crowd outside the stadium as everybody tried to find who they were related to. Angelina and I and some of our study buddies stuck close to each other instinctively in the throng. After looking around for a while, I saw my family coming toward us.

If the students had been enthusiastic with their hugs and handshakes and tears, my crew took it to the next level. I was all but tackled by half a dozen black men and women, then surrounded by several more.

"Hawk!" Karlie screamed, the way a teenage girl does when she's really psyched up. "You did it! And look at these!" she played with my *cum laude* cords.

Angelina and the others stood behind me, wide-eyed and wondering, looking at the assortment of folks who came to see me.

My biological dad and I stared at each other across a chasm of years. He'd gotten my mother pregnant and then refused any responsibility, too wrapped up in becoming an OG to intervene when she took me to crack houses, lost the house she'd shared with Charles, fought me in back-alley tournaments like an animal. Later in his life, when he was more established, he'd had two more kids by another woman. *Those* kids, I was told, he took care of. He was involved in their lives, in taking care of their mother.

Still, I had invited him. It was important. To see one of his kids - the first person in his family line - graduate from college. Maybe it would give him some hope. Maybe it would give hope to the half-siblings I'd barely met, who lived in a hood like mine.

In the end, he pulled me into an awkward hug - the kind you give when you're not sure what else to do. The kind that said he was sorry, that he knew he'd messed up.

Meanwhile, Angelina and her whole crew were having, I think, kind of a revelation. I'd been their classmate, their study buddy, every bit as diligent and high-achieving as they were. They'd figured that my hard work removed me from my background - removed me from the hood - and made me kind of like them.

Now they were staring at my homies and realizing, I'd been one of them, a hood kid, all along too. They were realizing that university honor students and the hood kids were really not such different species - you could be both at once, and flawlessly so.

My classmates and my homies stared at each other, staring past me like they were looking through a thick glass wall. They'd thought they were two different species before - but now, I belonged to both.

Angelina pushed her way to stand beside me, shoulder-to-shoulder. She reached across the chasm to shake my homies' hands.

"Hi," she said. "I'm Angelina. You must be Hawk's friends."

PIPE DREAMS

In reality I hated living pipe dreams
Serving poison to my people for some nice things

Sometimes, when I drove past that same gas station where my mother jumped out of my car for the last time, I saw Richard.

Richard was about my age, but he looked older. His life had been even tougher than mine. We'd been hustlers together back when I was a kid - but he was never gonna run more than a street corner. In time, he lost the ability to run even that. It was because his brain was shot to hell.

It wasn't cause of drugs. Richard never touched the stuff. It was because of something that was in the dirt, the wallpaper, the water coming out of his home's faucet.

It was because of lead.

Maybe you didn't know they used to make everything out of lead. It was cheap and it had some useful qualities, so it went into paint, wallpaper, lipstick, toys, gasoline, water pipes. Pretty much anything.

You probably don't know they used to do that 'cause they

stopped doing it when they found out it kills people. And does lots of nasty things before it kills them. Especially to kids.

Lead is what they call a neurotoxin. It damages the brain and nerves. Especially kids, if they grow up with lead in their food and water. Kids' brains grow fast, and if they're getting poisoned, they can lose a whole lot of IQ points and be real clumsy, just like Richard always ways. If kids' brains get pumped full of lead while they're growing, the effects never go away.

It also turns out, nobody ever cared enough to remove all the lead they put into poor neighborhoods. The residents sure as hell weren't gonna pay to install new pipes, treat or change the dirt in the yards, and remove all the old paint in their houses. Rich folks could do that kind of thing, and afford new houses that never had lead in the first place. But poor folks couldn't, and the government didn't consider that its problem.

How much lead poisoning you got, then, was largely a matter of luck. How much money did your family have?

Lead leaked out of old houses that were painted with lead inside and out. During the years when lead was used in gasoline, it got sprayed into the air by car exhaust and settled in the dirt of front yards where kids played. One of the handful of days when I did go to the school by McDonough Street, I found signs taped up next to the drinking fountains and sinks:

DO NOT DRINK. HAND WASHING ONLY.

I asked a teacher about it, and she said: "Oh, that. Well, there's lead in the water all around here. It's bad for your brain, you know? We aren't allowed to let you drink the water - but we haven't been able to replace the pipes. So bring water with you to school, okay?"

My house probably had the same lead pipes as the school, but the government didn't see that as a problem, and there was nothing the teachers could do about it.

My family was lucky in one big way, though. There was no lead paint in our house. Nolita's parents had helped her and Charles move into a new house - one that was built and painted after regulations on lead. New houses could still be hooked up to old, lead-ridden city plumbing. But they weren't painted with it.

Richard wasn't so lucky. I remember sitting with him one time on a stoop, keeping a lookout for some hustlers - and watching him pick up little flakes of paint from the door frame of this old house and eat them.

"Richard," I asked, with all the disgust my little ten-year-old self could muster, "what the hell you doing?"

"They're sweet," he explained, his speech a little slow like always. "Like candy. Can you believe it, these old houses just painted with sweet stuff. It's great when you're hungry. Try it." He held out a finger, sticky with paint chips and the sheen of his own saliva.

I scooted away. "Nah man, I'm good." And I stared as he ate the chips himself.

That's another problem. Turns out, lead *does* taste sweet. It makes a chemical called lead acetate, which is even sweeter than sugar. The old-school chemists called it "sugar of lead."

Years later, we found out Richard got a settlement for lead poisoning from the state. It turned out his house was particularly bad, plumbing-wise, and when his father got custody of the kids he took them all to get tested for lead in their blood. They got off-the-chart results. The state sent some inspectors to Richard's mom's home and measured the tap water. That shit was toxic waste-level bad.

It was so bad that Richard's dad's lawyers successfully argued that the state should never have let it get like that. That the state had *some* responsibility to stop children from getting poisoned, especially from public infrastructure like water pipes.

It turns out a lot of kids got settlements like that, from my part of Baltimore. It was money that was supposed to be dispersed across the course of the kid's life, to make up for the money they couldn't earn themselves because of the brain damage.

Problem was, that money didn't come with any built-in legal or financial advice. Soon after the state started paying these settlements out, predatory law firms popped up. "We'll get you *all* your money now," they said, "and you don't have to pay us anything. We'll only take a chunk of what we win for you. It's your money, after all - you should be able to do what you want with it, right now."

Of course, they'd take a *big* chunk. And they didn't care what happened afterward. Richard went to them, got all his money right away. The firm that got it for him took a huge chunk of it and gave him what was left.

He spent it all in a few years. And when I saw him, after my mother died, he was at a gas station begging for change.

Richard's story is real common. In cities around the country, there are these neighborhoods with lead paint, lead pipes, lead soil. Neighborhoods where scientists come in and say "don't grow nothing, the soil will make your plants poison." Neighborhoods where schools have "do not drink" signs by the drinking fountains, and kids eat flakes off the wall that taste like candy.

Almost all of these neighborhoods are majority black neighborhoods. There's a good reason for that, too. It's the same reason as all urban segregation.

You might have heard of redlining. Back in the day, that was where landlords, realtors, and banks would draw red lines on maps separating the "good" neighborhoods from the "bad" ones.

The logic was simple: only let white folks buy property in the "good" neighborhoods, 'cause that would keep the property values high. Realtors and landlords worried that white folks wouldn't pay as much for a house with a black family living next door. And white folks had all the money, so they figured the best way to get the highest prices for their properties was to not let black families move into any of the good neighborhoods.

Black folks, then, were only allowed to rent or buy in neighborhoods that already had crappy schools and high unemployment. The properties that no white folks in their right mind would want, the landlords figured, they could sell to black folks without losing any white people's money. That included almost all the neighborhoods with the poison in the dirt, with the peeling lead paint walls and the century-old lead pipes that no one had wanted to pay to replace.

If you look at a map of Baltimore that's color-coded by race, and then a map that's color-coded by high lead levels, the two maps are almost identical.

America's thinking a little more about lead than they used to, now, because of what's happening in Flint, Michigan.

In that city, the state governor hired someone to take over the city's utilities, thinking he could run it more efficiently than the local city council. The guy immediately decided it would be a great idea to make changes to the city's drinking water treatment. "Fiscal responsibility," he said, all proud of himself for having found a way to save a few bucks. When safety experts warned him that this was a terrible idea, he figured they were science nerds and ignored them.

Well, turned out the "changes" he made let loose a public health disaster so bad that the United Nations started making statements on it. Under the new protocols, the city's old lead pipes simply started to melt.

Water came out of Flint's taps the color of beer. A local car company stopped using the water in its manufacturing, because it was eating away at their car engine parts. For months, the state government told Flint's - mostly black - residents that it was fine, that the water was safe to drink. But at the same time, the state bussed in bottled water for state employees to drink at work.

Finally, somebody got some federal water testers out there. They were horrified by what they found. Just like in Richard's home, the water coming out of those taps literally qualified as toxic waste. Doctors started testing the blood of kids in Flint, and, no surprise - they found sky-high lead levels there, too.

It got real bad. It's still real bad.

The government of Michigan insisted it doesn't have the money to fix the problem, so most people living in Flint still don't have safe water.

The state government doesn't seem to care. A state nurse told one Flint mom about her kids: "It's only a few IQ points. Tt's not the end of the world."

But Flint might not be completely alone in this.

Some of the early tests of Flint's water - which government officials used as "proof" that the water was okay to drink - used "cheating" methods. They only measured water in ways and places that had less lead than the average Flint tap. They didn't want to have to deal with the cost of replacing the pipes, or switching to a more expensive water source, so they cheated.

Once it was discovered that this was happening in Flint, some journalists with The Guardian newspaper wondered if other cities with lead pipes might be doing the same thing.

Sure enough, 33 of the 43 major American cities whose methods they studied were cheating - using methods that suggested they were worried about lead in the drinking water in some parts of their cities, not all. They were worried enough to cheat to avoid revealing the truth. But not worried enough to replace the pipes in poor neighborhoods.

Lead in American cities is a huge problem - and not a surprising one, given that we built so many of our cities and made so much industrial waste before we knew much about poison.

Unfortunately, it's also a problem that affects mainly black folks, whose parents and grandparents were not allowed to rent or buy property in newer, safer neighborhoods until the past few decades.

And it is almost exclusively a problem that affects the poor, regardless of color. If rich folks don't like the water quality or the paint job in a neighborhood, they can just move, or pay to have it fixed.

Poor folks, though, are stuck. They can't move to neighborhoods with higher rent and property values, they can't pay to replace their city's pipes, and because they aren't cash cows for taxes, frankly, city and state governments don't care that much about them.

That has to change. I think about that every time I see Richard rattling his change jar. He's thirty, brain-damaged, and unemployable. Not considered smart enough to hold down a job; not considered disabled enough for disability. He's one of the people, like so many others, that fall through the cracks in a society that often only cares how much money a person is worth.

He grew up a few blocks from me, and my brothers and sisters. He went to the same schools, played in the same parks. Only difference was, our house was newer. A little pricier, thanks to Nolita's parents.

I guess we just got lucky.

BEAUTIFUL NOLITA, REPRISED

December 31st 's the day I lost my mother

I cried tears of pain

'cause I ain't tell her that I love her

After my mother jumped out of my moving car to avoid seeing her daughter in the hospital, I saw her one more time.

It was a beautiful spring day when I sat down at my computer. Since graduation I'd been running the property management business with Jordan - the one we started with legit money from selling shoes, of all things - and plotting how to make the world a better place.

I'd started mentoring kids from my old neighborhoods, and others like them. Kids who had probably never seen a wealthy black man who wasn't a hustler in person. I'd been going out to schools, making speeches, telling the little dudes and ladies about the world that awaited them if they mastered math and reading - worlds they'd never even seen.

I hadn't seen my mother, Nolita, in two years. Not since she broke me, broke my heart, refusing to see my sister after I'd fought three men and risked my life to get to her.

I'd come to peace with the fact that my mother, no matter how bad I wanted to save her, wasn't going to change. To change, a person has to want to change. And Nolita didn't.

I'd been focusing on my life, on what I could control, for months, and I was happy. I was happy when I opened my text inbox that day.

Then I saw the message:

Hawk. Did you know your mother's pregnant?

Pregnant. I stopped and tried to think about what that meant.

It meant another little me, growing up with Nolita. It meant another little me growing up in abandoned buildings with a mother much further gone than mine had been. Instead of a Charles, this kid would have a Heavy - an addict for a mom and an addict for a dad, and crack the only priority either of them had.

I went to see Nolita.

She and Heavy had moved, as is the way with addicts. They were living in a more-abandoned house now, in a more-abandoned neighborhood, and I relied on old contacts to find them.

The neighborhood was abandoned as in 'uncared for.' Windows were shuttered except where the shutters had fallen off off and no one had bothered to replace them. Paint peeled from siding, revealing dark, half-rotting wood underneath. Shingles were missing.

But it wasn't abandoned as in 'empty.' Around the block, dozens of people milled - hustlers, users, lookouts, prostitutes, people who just knew them and were looking to catch some sort of break. They all looked like hell. Ain't nobody healthy in a neighborhood like this.

I drove up - this time in a less-obvious car. Nolita was sitting on the stoop of the old, broken steps leading up to her old, broken house.

She also looked old and broken. She was even skinnier than when I'd seen her last, skin hanging loose where her curves used to be. Her skin had paled and yellowed, like she wasn't healthy enough to make the color brown. Her hair was thin, dry, frazzled, kept out of her face by a dirty torn rag. It was obvious that she didn't care about her looks anymore. She only cared about crack.

She held a blunt in one hand, smoke rising from it like a burning building. In her other hand was a can of beer. I glanced next to her and saw the rest of the six-pack sitting next to her.

But something in her was still alive. Her belly was swollen with a baby, sticking out of her skinny frame like an oasis in a desert.

I sat in my car for a long minute, breathing.

What is the right reaction when you see a pregnant woman, smoking a joint and drinking alcohol right in front of you? What if that woman is your mother?

I got out of my car real slowly. She saw me - I knew she recognized me at this distance. She gave me that mad, cold, sidelong look. That look that was designed to make you think she didn't care. But she looked at me. And she didn't run.

I walked toward her.

"Ma," I said, and I heard my own voice sound like a wounded animal, "I know you ain't sitting here smoking and drinking while you're pregnant."

She took another drag on her joint. "Is that all you have to say?" The voice that used to turn heads was now scratchy and dry.

"Ma…" I opened my hands helplessly. What can you tell your mother about babies that she doesn't already know? Seized by a sudden rage, I lashed out and snatched the half-empty beer can from her hands. I crushed it in a tight, angry fist and flung it aside. Heard it skitter to a halt on the cement somewhere behind me.

The block had gotten real quiet. People were staring, now. I knew why. You didn't mess with Nolita.

My mother stood up. "I don't have time for this shit," she spat at me. "I don't have time to deal with your judgemental shit. I live my life the way I want to. I don't know why you people have such a problem with that."

"Ma, it's not *just* your life! It was my life, too."

My mother turned away and started to walk into the house.

I'd talked to Aunt Patty, once, about why Nolita had so many babies. Many women in her position - knowing they wanted no part of responsibility for a child - had their tubes tied.

But Nolita loved the *idea* of children. She loved the special treatment she got when she was pregnant. And more than that, looking back on my own childhood, I think she loved the idea of having a friend who wouldn't abandon her, no matter what she did to herself.

The friend's needs, the child's needs, were inconsequential. She couldn't bear to think about how they conflicted with her own. So she didn't.

I wanted to follow her. To grab her. To scream at her. I wanted to take the baby out of her belly and take it home with me.

But I couldn't. And I couldn't disrespect my mother.

Instead, I whirled. Looked at the staring people, the hustlers, the buyers, the enablers.

"You'll do anything for money!" I screamed. "How are you selling drugs to pregnant women? How are you giving her alcohol? If I ever see any of you selling my ma drugs while she's pregnant - I'm coming for you!"

My vision started to go red. It was like being in the ring again.

"I'll kill you, you hear! I'll kill anyone who sells drugs to my mother!"

Amazingly, there were cooler heads on the block than mine.

One of the women came up to me. She was a mother herself. More of a mother than mine. You could tell by the way she moved, by the way she spoke to calm me down like a frightened child. She was skinny herself, a user, but not too far gone to have lost sight of the world.

"Hawk," she said, "this is what your mother wants. You can't keep fighting us over what she wants to do. You can't keep fighting *yourself* over what she wants to do. The hustlers here could stop selling to her, sure. You know what she'd do then? She'd move. She'd move until she found somebody who would sell to her. She'd move until she lost you, if she had to. You can't keep fighting us over what she'll do no matter what."

I cried. That lady came and put her arms around me, and I held her. Just like she was my ma. I realized then that I had never held Nolita as an adult, never held her to this body. Every time I saw her, we were fighting. We were afraid to get close to each other.

I left that day, still crying. Knowing I could not, would not see her again.

☆☆☆

The next time I heard about my mother I was sitting at my coffee table, reading.

I recognized the hospital's number. They used the same caller ID for all their outgoing calls. I'd last seen that caller ID when Delilah was hospitalized, four years earlier.

I picked up the call, my heart pounding.

"Hawk?"

"Yeah?"

"We have your mother here. You're listed as one of her emergency contacts."

"Is she okay?"

"You should get here as soon as possible."

I don't know how I got to the hospital. In one piece, that is. I drove faster than I ever have in my life - dodging and weaving between lanes, car tires squealing around corners. Looking back, I was in no condition to be driving.

I was a terrified mess.

The nurses wouldn't take me to see her right away. It was her lungs, they said. Her lungs were eaten up by decades of smoking crack.

'Damaged' was the word they used. Clinical, scientific. But I remembered those anti-smoking ads they'd shown us in high school. If smoking cigarettes would make your lungs black and swollen and useless, what would smoking crack do?

I didn't want to know.

She'd had something like an asthma attack, they said. No medicine on hand, 'cause she hadn't seen a doctor or been to a pharmacy in years. At some point, she simply stopped breathing. It took the folks around her a while to notice.

I later learned that Heavy called the ambulance. But he'd been so visibly upset that the EMTs had tried to keep him at a distance. Then he'd disappeared. Ran, I figured. So he wasn't there, didn't know, when she was -

When she was declared dead on arrival.

I plunked myself down in a chair beside the nurses and stared at the floor.

Dead.

In your mind, you always think you'll see your mother again.

She's been with you since before you were born, and you figure she always will be. No matter how stupid or hurtful her decisions, she's a part of the background of your life. Always there.

"Would you like to see her?"

I nodded. I didn't know what to expect.

My mother's body was laid out on a cold metal slab. She was cold too, and still. It had only been two years since I saw her last, sitting on that stoop, but she seemed to have aged ten. Her hair was grey, and missing in places, her face a mess of wrinkles and lines. Her limbs were bone-thin. Open boils and sores had dried when her heart stopped beating. She wasn't yet fifty.

"That's not my mother," I heard myself saying.

In my mind I saw the mother I remembered from my childhood. The one I had looked up to. I saw her flawless brown complexion, her supermodel skills with makeup and clothing. I saw the way she swaggered her hips the day she met Charles, heard the sass in her voice that never failed to make others pay attention.

Love was the profession my mother had chosen, and she had dominated it, hooking man after man on her the way she was hooked on drugs. It wasn't the path I would have chosen. But my mother was like me in one way. What she did, she did well. And what she did, when I knew her, was be *beautiful.*

"That's not my mother," I said again.

I wondered, right then, how my mother's life would've been if she hadn't been raped as a child. How it would have been if she had gone to a school that understood her. I pictured her in a salon, running first chair, making other women look beautiful. I pictured her reading to me after school.

But it was all over. None of that was going to happen. It was never going to. I'd always known, somewhere deep down, that her addiction would kill her. Dying before fifty wasn't unusual for an addict. I'd seen plenty of "old" men and women disappear, stop coming for new hits when I was a hustler. You hoped they got arrested or hospitalized, that they had a roof over their head. But you knew they probably hadn't.

My mother's family started arriving soon after.

I wanted a closed casket funeral. I knew Nolita would have hated being seen the way she was now. She looked nothing like the mother I had known growing up. The body she left behind was emaciated, most of her hair and flesh gone, dry skin hanging off her bones like she was a famine victim. I knew that no amount of makeup would make her look like she had before. Like a completely different person.

But I didn't have power of attorney. That was my mother's sister, who insisted that we doll Nolita's sad little broken body up as best we could and put it on display. She said that people deserved to see Nolita one last time. That they deserved to say goodbye.

I made my feelings known, tried to protect my mother like I always had. But it didn't make a difference. My mother wasn't here to speak for herself, anymore.

Even with a wig and fresh makeup and fancy clothes, she looked nothing like the pictures her sister propped up by the casket. Pictures of Nolita young and round and glowing. This body still looked like it belonged to someone else. Someone that Nolita would never have wanted to be. That was who she was in the end, I guess. Someone she didn't want to be.

The church was full for the funeral. My mother had known everyone, and even those who didn't *like* her were drawn into the orbit of her magnetism. My mother's siblings and their children. Aunt Patty and her children. Heavy and Charles and my biological father came. All my siblings - a small herd of people from my age down to toddlerhood who shared one parent or the other with me. OGs and hustlers from miles around, big-deal OGs who were rarely seen on the street anymore. So many people brought flowers that they had to start piling them outside of the church's doors.

I didn't know what to say. I didn't know what to feel or think. This was my mother, but she was also the woman who had refused to protect me from herself. And these were her friends, her family, but half of them had also helped kill her.

There's nothing to say. No simple answers. The problem is bigger than any one person's mind could solve.

Why was Nolita raped as a child? Why did the same thing happen to her mother? Why were the girls who reported the rape told to keep it quiet to preserve men's reputations? Why was Nolita offered crack instead of justice?

Why were we *all* offered crack instead of justice?

On our way out, I heard the whispers.

What happened to Nono? Are you sure that was her?

That didn't look like Nono to me.

What happened? She used to be so pretty...

Nolita's sister met my eyes as we stood across from each other at the doors of the church, thanking guests for coming on their way out. After a minute, she bowed her head a little. *You were right,* her eyes said, sadly. But it was too late now: everyone had seen Nolita the way she was at the end.

I left that day having learned nothing new. I'd known what was happening all along. The only thing I learned was the power of my mother's magnetism - so many people turned out to honor her, who honored no one but herself.

Maybe people needed someone like that - someone who believed in their own choices so much it gave them something to believe in, too.

I thought that the funeral, where I saw that sad, skinny body in that fancy suit, would be the last I would see of my mother. I thought that chapter of my life had closed.

I was wrong, in a way I could never have imagined.

There would be a chance for redemption that I never saw coming.

ELIJAH

After my mother's funeral, I returned to my life in a daze.

Charles was right. I couldn't save her. But now - I no longer worried about her. As much as she'd looked worn and sick, my mother also looked relaxed in that coffin. She was free of what the world had been doing to her. She was at peace.

With my mother gone, there was no reason for me to go back to the old neighborhood. I was surprised, then, to get a call from an old friend who lived out there.

"Hawk," she said, "do you know your little brother is in one of the abandoned houses out here?"

I paused.

"...what?"

"His mom's dead and his dad's missing. He's just all by himself in this crack house."

"All by himself...what is he, two years old?"

"Something like that."

I almost dropped the phone. Then I pretty much ran outside

and threw myself into my car.

The house my contact sent me to was a broken-down mess. It was the place I'd last seen Nolita and Heavy - but apparently, neither of them were here now.

I walked up the creaking steps and into the sound of somebody - a few somebodies, actually - having sex on a threadbare sofa in the front room. Other skinny bodies were splayed out on cardboard boxes and old blankets, nodding, sleeping, twitching. The familiar smell of urine and feces mixed with body odor and kitchen chemicals wafted past me. I took a deep breath. I had so many memories of places like this - none of them good.

In the kitchen, sunlight filtered through the gaps in the boards that had been nailed over the windows.

There, by the trash can, I saw a kid.

A baby, really. He was standing up, but just barely. He was dirty, wearing a soiled diaper, and reaching up as high as he could to try to pull scraps of food out of the garbage.

My stomach flipped over.

The rage was back. I had a flashback of when I saw Nolita drinking and smoking with the poor kid in her belly. Worse. How far gone did you have to be to ignore a starving child?

Stilling my pulse as best I could, I approached the little guy and squatted down beside him.

"Hey little man," I said softly. "What's your name?"

He stopped and looked at me. "Dada?"

My stomach flipped again. "No...no I'm not your daddy. We're gonna find your daddy. What's your name?"

He looked at me for a moment, blinking.

"Okay then." I looked at his puffy, dirty diaper, at the food and grease smeared on his skin from feeding himself out of the trash. "Let's get you cleaned up," I whispered.

The house had no running water, so I put him in my car and drove to the hospital. I drove so fast, I almost ran a couple of lights.

When I walked into the hospital, I was met by cold stares.

"Are you his father?" a nurse asked me with a chilly gaze, holding out her hands for the baby. She looked like she wanted to take him from me, and never give him back.

"No! No way I would've let him get like this. I'm his brother. His mom - our mom - just died. I thought his dad had him, but somebody called me and said his dad's missing. I came out to get him and -" I looked at her helplessly.

The nurse pursed her lips. I handed the little guy over, reluctantly, and went to check him in.

I was in luck. This was the same hospital the kid had been born at. Their records said his name was Elijah, the child of one Nolita. Their records confirmed that I was also Nolita's son, so they let me walk back and stay with Elijah while the nurses washed him in a little basin.

"You're his brother," one of them said softly, as they dried him off. "Not his father?"

"No ma'am. His daddy...well, I've gotta find his daddy."

"Well, that does make things difficult. If you're not his parent or guardian, we can't release him to go home with you. We have to give him to a foster family until his real parents can be found."

Memories of my time in foster care came flooding back. I tried to imagine my first family - the one with the hot spoons - being trusted with a toddler.

But I also remembered the requirements for foster parenting. I remembered what my Aunt Patty and my Grandmother had had to do to get me, what Charles had been unable to do.

"What if I qualified as a foster parent?" I asked her.

The nurse raised her eyebrows at me.

"Yeah. My aunt fostered me when I was younger. What if I met all the requirements to be a foster parent, and I registered with the system? Could I take him home then? You know - until we find his daddy?"

The nurse glanced uneasily at the little boy, who was looking anxiously around from his seat on the hospital bed.

"Let me ask our social work department. We'd have to place him somewhere else for a few days while the paperwork goes through. But if you can get certified...I think that just might work."

★★★

I'd never worked so fast in my life.

The first thing I had to do was get an apartment that met foster care standards. That meant a separate bedroom for the little man. Fortunately, as the co-owner of a property management business, finding a two-bedroom apartment for rent wasn't hard.

I had my furniture moved, bought a crib and some toys, toddlers' clothes, baby books, and diapers. The whole nine yards. I made sure everything was childproofed and cleaned the whole place like I was washing my favorite car.

It felt like my whole apartment was preparing for a job interview - which was exactly what was happening.

Within two days, I was ready. Wearing my best crisp, clean pants and dress shirt, I invited the social workers in.

They looked at everything, pencils poised above their clipboards, taking notes.

"You are this child's brother, is that correct?"

"Yes, ma'am."

"You know that means the state will not be able to provide you with a stipend for his care, correct?"

"Yes, ma'am. That won't be a problem."

"Have you ever cared for a small child before?"

"My siblings, ma'am. I'm the oldest of seven. I took care of all of them at Elijah's age."

The social workers eyed me, and went over the place with a fine-toothed comb.

I knew the job I'd done preparing for my little brother was legit. The visibly surprised social workers agreed. They had come in ready to be judgemental, but I watched the tension melt as they went through Elijah's crib, his closet, and the diapers under the bathroom sink. By the time they wrapped up, they were smiling. I could tell I was one of their easy jobs.

"Elijah is very lucky to have a brother like you."

"Thank you, ma'am. I do my best."

"When would be a good time for you to pick Elijah up from the family that is taking care of him?"

"How about right now?"

☆☆☆

Settling in with my little man was a strange mix of joy and terror.

I'd cared for little kids before - but it had been a while, and I had only been a kid myself. Back then, there was no option but for me to do what no one else would. I'd had no concept of what a good parent was. Anything was better than nothing, and nothing was what they were getting without me.

With Elijah, though, I had role models to measure myself against. I had Charles. I had Aunt Patty.

Next to them, I felt like I had no idea what I was doing.

Elijah was scared of his own shadow at first. I didn't want to think too hard about why that might be. No one knew how long he'd been alone in that house, or how far gone Heavy and Nolita were before she died.

It was clear that safety was foreign to him. He got scared when I first put him in the crib, so I stayed with him until he fell asleep. He was scared when I first put him in a high chair, and fought against it, so I made funny faces and shapes with his food until he got the idea that the high chair meant food.

He ate an unbelievable amount. For the first few weeks I figured that was normal - I didn't know how long he'd been without food. But no amount of regular meals seemed to convince him that food was going to keep coming. He would stuff food in his diaper and then hide it in his room, preparing little food stores he hid so well it took me months to find all of them.

The state ordered me to take Elijah to a psychiatrist up at the hospital. By the time the first appointment came, I was all for that. Elijah was clearly scared all the time. He cried and whined whenever I left the room. He kicked and screamed when I tried to dress him. He woke up at night crying and screaming, sending me running in my pajamas to calm him down.

The psychiatrist asked me what I knew about his past. As Elijah played with some toys, temporarily distracted, I told him all I could guess.

I told him how it had been for me with my mother - how I'd fed my little siblings more than she did in the midst of her crack haze. About how my mother couldn't even feed herself at the end, how it got so bad that she died. How his father, presumably, had been there when it happened. How he'd taken no responsibility.

The psychiatrist took notes, his face getting grimmer and grimmer. "How long," he asked finally, "do you expect to have Elijah?"

That question made everything get real quiet inside my head.

It wasn't like I hadn't thought of it before. But I'd been avoided it for a reason. My whole life had changed since I took in

Elijah. I had no time to be *me* anymore. I hadn't even had nine months' warning before suddenly becoming a single parent.

I'd been telling myself that I'd find Heavy, make him take responsibility. The man used to be an OG, right? He could handle shit. I'd give Heavy a few months to shape up his life, and then -

But the truth was, that was just like dreaming of Nolita getting better. I never really wanted to give Elijah to that man.

I didn't want to trust my little brother to anyone else.

☆☆☆

We got into a routine. I managed the property business from home as much as I could, bringing my little man with me whenever I had to go out. He spent the day running around the apartment like a tiny maniac while I did business from home. Sometimes I tried reading to him, but he was usually more interested in grabbing the book and feeling the texture of its pages than in sitting still and listening.

In time, I got used to the idea of hiring babysitters, of finding a daycare. I convinced myself that someone else - a qualified professional - could watch Elijah while I kept the business going.

I then learned that I wasn't the only one who thought he was a hyper little dude. A smiling but exhausted day care teacher met me at the end of his first day. She said Elijah had three times the energy of her other children.

I thought of Nolita. Nolita, who'd had such a hard time sitting through classes in school that she was constantly in trouble. Who was told she was a bad student, that there was something wrong with her.

And in the back of my mind I wondered what would happen when they found Heavy. I kept telling myself I would wait another day before going back down to the hood to look for him. Truth was, I was terrified to see him. Scared to hear that he wanted Elijah; scared to hear that he didn't.

Jordan and my family were understanding of my sudden single dad lifestyle. Aunt Patty thought I'd make the perfect parent for Elijah. She told me not to fool myself that Heavy would make any kind of dad for him.

"If he could not take care of Nolita, what makes you think he can take care of a child?" she asked. "You know what Elijah has been through. And you know what you needed, at that age."

What I'd needed at Elijah's age was safety. Safety and love. Most of all, *love*. I remembered how my mother's disapproval had hurt more even than the edge of that wooden step.

I resolved never to let Elijah feel that way. Ever.

When I got a phone call from an unknown Baltimore number, I picked it up anxiously. I thought it might be someone from the foster care system.

Instead, there was a strained, cracked man's voice on the other end of the line.

"Hawk? This is Heavy. I need to see you."

☆☆☆

I drove up to the address Heavy gave me on the phone. Parked my car, and looked around warily. This one wasn't in a populated part of the hood. It was on the outskirts, not a soul in sight. That was usually either a sign of an ambush, or of somebody who was hiding.

I got out of my car slowly, carefully, keeping a sharp eye out.

I climbed the rickety, rotting wooden stairs at the front of the house and banged on the door. When it didn't open right away, I banged again. "Heavy? It's Hawk."

The door opened a crack. Heavy's bloodshot eye peered out at me. Just from the sliver of his face I could see, it was clear he'd lost at least fifty pounds since we last spoke.

The door opened more, and I saw the hand Heavy laid against the door frame. It was clutching a gun.

"Whoa, whoa," I put my hands out in front of me, open and empty. "What the hell you wavin' that thing around for? You wanna get someone killed?"

Heavy's face cracked. Everything about him seemed cracked - his dry, husky voice, his dark, deeply wrinkled and sagging skin. Now it was a bitter grimace that split his face, baring his teeth. I realized he was crying.

"Yeah, man. Yeah, I kind of do."

But from the way he lowered the gun, I could tell it wasn't me he wanted to do in. I followed him into the house, slowly and carefully.

"They're out to get me, man," he said, too quickly, leading me into a room with some broken down furniture. "Shit's gettin' crazy - you can't be too careful."

Inside, the house was dark but for light seeping from the shutters. It smelled like Heavy had been living there a while, and hadn't bothered to invest in running water.

"Hawk," he told me, not looking at me, plunking himself into the decrepit ruin of an armchair, "I can't live without your mother." A sob shook him. "I...messed up. I let her get too sick. How could she leave us? She was supposed to fight!"

"Hard to fight an asthma attack," I said quietly. "Hard to fight anything when you can't get no air in your lungs."

He seemed not to have heard me. He waved the gun around, more talking with his hands than pointing it at anything. "Your mother was - was everything. You know it, Hawk. I remember you tried to save her as hard as I did. You tried to save her even when I couldn't get it right. Hell, you fought me over it. So you understand. You understand that you can't - you can't just *lose* Nolita."

Heavy took a couple of deep, ragged breaths.

"I can't do this shit without your mother. I'm about to kill myself." Heavy waved the gun again, and before I could react, he'd stuck it all the way into his mouth.

"Whoa! Whoa, whoa. You don't gotta be doin' that!" I walked toward him slowly, my hands outstretched again, like I was trying to calm a spooked animal.

He hadn't pulled the trigger yet - which I guessed meant he wasn't going to. But I had no idea what I'd do if he did.

"You don't gotta be doing that," I soothed, like I was soothing Elijah. "I know my Ma meant a lot to a lot of people. But you've still got plenty to live for. Hell, you've got her son!"

Heavy looked at me, and his eyes unfocused for a minute. Finally he let his hand drop to his side, the gun held limply in it. I swooped in fast and took it from him, like I was taking a toy from Elijah. He let me have it.

I stood there, staring. He looked almost like my mother, sitting here, broken, in an empty house. I remembered my mother curled up by candlelight on our living room floor, rocking as she waited for her next fix.

Part of me wanted to take over, to take care of him, to take his whole goddamn family under my wing like I would have done for Nolita years ago.

But he also looked like the man who helped kill her. The man who kept feeding her drugs, too blind to see what they were doing. The man who abandoned Elijah in a crack den because he couldn't think beyond his own addiction.

My eyes filled up with tears. "Heavy, what the *hell?* You're supposed to be the man here. You were supposed to be *Nolita's* man. How much crack did you give her on the day she died?"

Heavy recoiled from me, the way I used to recoil from my mother's yelling. The words poured out of me.

"Do you remember *Elijah?* Your son? Who did you think was feeding him? Or changing his dirty diapers? How do you run away from that?"

Heavy gestured around the dark, empty room. "I can't do shit for Elijah. You know that. Your ma trusted me to take care of her and her kid, and look where that got her. I can't do shit for anybody, Hawk. I'm too far gone."

I stared at him. "You're not even gonna *try?*"

"I can't, Hawk. I can't. I'm barely keepin' myself alive. What do you think will happen if you give me a baby? You really want to go down that road?"

Too angry to speak, I realized I was still clutching Heavy's gun. I emptied the chamber and hurled it away, into a dark corner, like it had burned me. Then I turned and left.

I walked out of that empty house, down those rickety steps, and pulled out in my car. My blood was running hot, my vision threatening to turn red. I had to keep it together. I couldn't afford to do anything stupid.

Heavy was right about one thing. Elijah didn't deserve Heavy.

He deserved a good father.

☆☆☆

With Heavy still alive but unfit to take Elijah, Elijah and I were left in limbo.

Legally, a foster parent has to wait two years before beginning the adoption process, unless both of the child's parents are deceased. The parents have two years to try to get their act together and get their kid back.

Part of me hoped Heavy would turn his life around and become a good father to Elijah. Hoped that someday I'd go visit them both, living in a nice, big Aunt Patty style house with nice sitcom neighbors.

Another part of me *knew* I was dreaming.

What I was not expecting was the call I got two months later, from the same neighbor who had told me about Elijah.

"Hawk." There was a long silence on the line. Too long. "Heavy's dead. The house he was stayin' in burned down. They found a body inside. They can't ID it yet because it's too burned up, but it's gotta be him. No one has seen him since the fire."

I was almost calm as I got a babysitter for Elijah, got into my car, and drove back to the place where I saw Heavy last.

It almost felt like I had never left. Like the house had just burned down in front of me, the match lit by Heavy's own hand.

The scene was a pile of black rubble. Caution tape had been unspooled all around the scene, blowing in the breeze like some morbid decoration.

A man and a woman in plain clothes - detectives, I was guessing - were casing it when I showed up.

As I drove up, they tensed visibly. So I got out of the car with my empty hands held up in plain sight, with a walk that I hoped said I was friendly. They didn't go for the guns at their belts, so I approached them slowly.

"Hey," I said. "I'm Hawk. My - stepfather - was staying at this house. Nobody's seen him since the fire. Do you know what happened here?"

"Are you his next of kin?"

"I guess so. My mother - his wife - died two months ago. I'm fostering his son right now. I was - kinda hoping he'd get it together, hoping he would work to be the father he should have been. This, though..." I looked back at the charred remains.

The detectives glanced at each other. "We don't know where your stepfather is. Only one body was found here, and we haven't been able to identify it yet."

"Yeah. Some folks from the neighborhood told me a body had been found. When will you know if it's him?"

"We'll have to run the bones against dental records and see if there's a match." The detective's voice softened, seeing how I stared at what was left of the house. "That will take - no more than two weeks. In the meantime, I'm afraid this house is a crime scene. We can't have anyone going in there, tampering with the evidence."

I glanced up from the bed of charcoal. "A crime scene? You're sure it wasn't an accident?"

"The victim - whoever it was - was already dead before the fire started. We don't think it was self-inflicted."

I stuck my hands in my pockets. I wasn't shocked. I shouldn't even have been surprised. Almost all hustlers die from another hustler's bullet, if they don't get life in prison first. But I'd been away from the violence long enough, almost, to forget. I walked away from that house with a strange feeling in my stomach.

Heavy had done it on purpose.

I was sure he had. He'd stolen from some hustler, or stepped in their territory, on purpose. That way he could tell himself he didn't pull the trigger.

☆☆☆

The dental records confirmed it. The bullet-riddled body in the house was Heavy, following Nolita into the next life.

With both Elijah's parents deceased, the social workers told me I needed a permanence plan. I needed to start adoption proceedings, to become Elijah's father for life - or give him to someone who would.

I sat on the couch that night, looking at my little man.

Nothing had been the same since he came into my life. My daily schedule was devoted to Elijah's security, happiness, and health. There were the weekly visits to his psychiatrist, social worker meetings twice a month. There was staying up late into the night with him crying, flailing, screaming like he thought he was back with Nolita again.

Going from free-wheeling fly bachelor to single dad in the space of an instant was a lot. It would mean a total change to my expectations for my life.

But in a way, it was exactly what I'd always wanted.

Once, I'd wanted to have the power to take care of Nolita. I'd pictured myself a grown man, fantasized about being a hustler so I could give my ma anything she needed. I'd tried and tried to save her from the streets, up to sabotaging my own happy life with Aunt Patty because my mother said she needed me. Up to risking everything by fighting Heavy and his customers as a grown-ass man.

Elijah was Nolita's son. I could give him everything. Everything I'd ever wanted to give her, her mother, my own younger self. Sitting beside his crib at night, knowing I could provide for him, gave me a kind of peace I'd never gotten from stacks of cash.

I wanted to keep him.

I looked at the little baby running around my apartment a mile a minute like he was on caffeine, and I knew I wanted to keep him. I could not imagine giving him to anyone else.

☆☆☆

It took two years for Elijah to stop hiding food. Two years to really understand that he was safe, that I wasn't gonna disappear and abandon him to starve. He still eats until he can't eat anymore, then asks for more if he thinks there is any.

The scars of those first two years run deep. But I like to think he won't remember them - not consciously, anyway, just like I don't remember my good years with Nolita before she found crack.

Today, he's happy. A sweet, smiling, happy kid. Other kids love him, and so do teachers. Except, sometimes, for one thing.

Elijah has never lost his hyperactive energy. He started first grade this year - and to this day he wakes up at 5am and starts running around the house, grabbing everything that he can grab, learning about the world through his hands.

Watching him, I can see how smart he is. I also can't picture him ever sitting quietly in front of a blackboard all day.

In the first year, Elijah was kicked out of two day care programs because of his energy. The teachers said they loved him, that there wasn't a mean bone in his body - but that they couldn't handle him when they had a dozen other children to watch.

That first year I got phone calls, sometimes more than once a week, begging me to come pick Elijah up or just wanting to vent about the fact that he would not sit still.

So for the next two years, I took him everywhere with me.

He came with me to meetings, to my talks when I gave motivational speeches. He came with me when we were showing clients properties and when I had dinners out with Jordan. He became my happy little whirlwind of activity - a bright young mind, drinking in the world with the same bottomless appetite he has for food. That's what his energy is, I think. An appetite for life.

In the last year before he started elementary school, I became a certified teacher. I began to teach full-time, at the same school that Elijah attended. Other teachers can't handle my little man. But I can. And even now, I'm always on call for when he needs me.

Elijah keeps me busy, but I can imagine no more meaningful job.

I wonder, sometimes, what might have happened to Nolita if she had had a parent like me, a teacher like me. A school like Elijah's that understands that every child is different. Would she have been told so often that she was a bad child, a worthless student, an irredeemable failure? Would she have skipped school so often, given up any ambition of having a career?

Would I have done the same, if I had gone to a school that told me the same things?

Elijah is my life. Kids like him, kids like me, are my life. Children need to be taken care of. If we're not cared for as kids, what happens?

The street life, the drug game. We try to fill the holes inside ourselves with money, drugs, sex. We know those things will kill us young, but nothing else worth having seems within our grasp -so we just try to live as fast as we can.

Now is the time to change that.

We all know what we need. You look around you, you know what your brothers and sisters need. We've got to take care of each other, if we ever want real peace. The kind of peace I have with Elijah.

My little man will not be like his mother, or his father, or his grandmother before him. He won't even be like me. He's going to grow up with love and support - the things I missed more than food when I was his age.

I've dedicated my life to Elijah. And to all of you who stand where I once stood, to all you kids from the hood. I dedicate my life to showing you what's possible for you, what really is within reach.

You can help. You can love and support each other. You can be good examples to each other.

I never thought I'd find myself where I am - a community leader, former- teacher, a father, a businessman. I never thought I'd stand on the stage at the University of Baltimore, or be someone that people pointed to as a good example for their kids.

But here I am. Taking care of my brother the way I always dreamed of taking care of my mother. Living the high life, but without the risk of prison time.

If I could do it, coming from where I came from, you can do it too.

I'll be thinking of you tonight, of all the little Hawks and Delilahs, as I take my little brother's hand and walk him home from school.

THE NOLITA PROJECT

A few days after my mother's funeral, I woke up with a mission burning through my veins.

Somewhere deep down, under all the 'thank yous' and 'I'm sorry's' I'd been giving out to friends and family members, something else was happening in me. I was remembering. Remembering, remembering. What life was like for me as a kid. For the young kids I looked after in my early hustling days. For Richard with his paint chips and the hood kids I'd seen in prison.

And somewhere in me, I couldn't let it happen anymore. I knew that my old neighborhood, countless other neighborhoods, were full of kids going through the same shit. Kids who feel like it's no reason to attend school, with barely any schools to go to, kids who had never seen a role model outside of the local hustlers who told them not to do drugs while flashing all the cash they made from it. Kids with no real adult parents, with parents who'd sell food for crack, with teachers who had so many kids to look after they couldn't even keep a head count.

I couldn't let it happen anymore.

I didn't think about long-term strategy. I just went out into the streets. The property business paid the bills, and I didn't have

Elijah at first, so I spent my time on the streets. At bus stops, at parks, on corners where I knew little hustlers worked. I talked to them about their feelings, and their families. I talked to them about their futures.

The kids didn't know what to make of me, at first. Wasn't normal for an adult to take an interest in them unless they wanted something from them. But I spoke their language, and I still had street cred in some places. And now I had another kind of cred. A college degree, a successful business that didn't involve killing people or getting shot.

Slowly, the kids started to take an interest in becoming like me.

When a former hustler asked them about their futures, they listened. They thought about it. They tell me their problems - why they aren't going to school, why they are failing school, why they can't get their homework done at home. I do everything I can to help those kids. To be the big brother me and mine had always needed.

Of course, you can probably predict the problems. A strange dude with no credentials wandering around talking to other people's children. Families weren't eager to let me in their houses. Ministers and teachers - the people who, I realized, could help me do even more good through churches and schools - didn't want to introduce the children they looked after to some random dude.

But I knew what to do about that. I knew business. What I needed was a credential, an organization that could be held accountable for my actions.

So I started the Nolita Project.

I named it that because it was for my mother. Not the woman who was cruel to me, but the little girl who was once kind to me. The little girl whose life might have been very different, who might not have been so desperately addicted, if she'd had more contact with adults who she could trust.

I'd gotten out safe, after all. My mother hadn't.

I didn't start the Nolita Project with any kind of big expansion plans. I just couldn't bear to sit still while I knew kids were out there getting into trouble that maybe they wouldn't be able to get out of.

But it worked like it always had: people recognized a good thing when they saw one. And I just happen to be a good thing.

With official credentials behind me, I could get into schools and churches. I could get principals and ministers to let me start spending time with their kids as a mentor. It was like a one-man Big Brothers Big Sisters operation: I'd talk to groups of kids, spend time with them after school, help them with their homework, help keep them entertained so they were off the streets.

After Elijah came into my life, I started volunteering at the school he went to, too. I worked with the older kids - the ones who were already facing big decisions in their lives.

The kids were always shocked that there was an adult who really understood them. They were so used to teachers telling them hilarious things like 'stay away from drugs.'

Well, here was somebody who knew all about drugs - who'd been successful at the game, and then gotten out of it to save my life. So when I talked about drugs, about school, about success, they listened.

Pretty soon one of those principals asked me to become a full-time, paid substitute teacher at his school. And then I started thinking. If somebody was willing to pay me to work with kids, even with public school budgets being what they were, what was to stop the Nolita Project from growing?

I contacted an old classmate from my college days - a dude named Jim who was a behavior specialist. As a behavior specialist, he worked with kids who had behavior problems, worked on finding ways for them to succeed. His work was right up my alley, and he knew a thing or two about educational programs and contracts.

Jim started helping me get contracts with schools all around Baltimore and D.C.. We started thinking about how we could invite people to give tax-deductible donations, what kinds of classes we could offer if we got a little funding.

The ideas started flowing. And pretty soon, so did the donations and the contract funding.

Today, the Nolita Project offers one-on-one mentoring and classes at three schools in the Baltimore/DC area.

There's our Media and Technology classes, where kids learn to use cameras, video editing software, learn to set up lighting and interview each other and make great-looking videos.

There's our tutoring, where our volunteer tutors help kids with their homework after school and during school hours, and even make home visits. Parents can sign kids up for mentoring to get their kids academic help, life advice, and a big brother who will even take them to the park or play video games with them if there's time.

One of my favorites is the Creative Writing classes. We teach kids to express themselves - really express themselves -

through poetry, spoken word performances, hip hop, and rap. We've even got partnerships with local sound engineers and music producers, who'll do things like send us royalty-free instrumental tracks from their studios. Our kids sing over them, turn them into songs about the things that are on their hearts.

The Nolita Project also gets people involved in their communities, through all sorts of community improvement events. In one annual event, we collect donations of new or gently used coats from local residents and department stores. Those go to homeless and low-income folks. We also hold neighborhood clean-ups, where kids and adults run around their neighborhoods picking up trash and making them look beautiful. When we see an opportunity to build community, we do it.

Now, I've got a new kind of street cred. Just like I was once known as a hustler, I'm now known as a mentor. As somebody who's been in the drug game, gotten out of it, who can speak to kids who are at risk of falling into it for that reason. I get invited to travel as a motivational speaker to all kinds of schools.

For the Nolita Project, this is just the beginning. I've always been good at growing operations - and I can see so many ways for this one to grow. By putting adults who know these kids, who care about them, in places where they can help, we can help build communities everywhere, and heal generations of trauma and injustice.

There are obstacles in our path. There always are. I know more about that than anyone. That's why the kids listen to me. Because when I tell them 'Don't give up,' when I tell them, 'You've got to keep pushing,' they listen, because I've done it myself.

I've come from the deepest pain you can imagine - from

generations of it, from wells so deep my mother couldn't escape. I've come from the drug war and the poverty and the abuse. I know all these things, and I've made a better life for myself. So when I tell people: 'Don't give up,'" they believe me.

And that's what I'm telling you now. It might feel overwhelming, to try to solve the problems I've talked about. But trying is the only way any problem has ever been solved. Trying is where all the good in the world comes from.

So I invite you - whether you're a kid, a parent, or somebody else - to join me in trying to help. Join me in trying to make a difference for those kids who might be facing what I once faced. Who might be in danger of falling into the traps that got my mother.

There are countless ways to help. The Nolita Project is one. If you like what we're doing, you can check out our website where you can apply to become a mentor like me, donate some funds, or buy our "I Deserve to Live" t-shirt for a young person you love.

But this book isn't an ad for an organization. It's a call to action. It's the idea that success is possible for all our kids - no matter what circumstances they come from. For the idea that we can heal our communities of the wounds of our past by coming together - as long as we keep trying.

If you're struggling with hurt and pain in your life, don't give up. Keep pushing. Amazing things are possible for you. I know it.

If your heart is breaking with the weight of the world, keep pushing. Keep trying. That's the only way we're ever gonna make things better.

That's what I remind myself every night as I tuck my little brother into bed.

My journey doesn't stop here and neither does yours. I believe that in order to change the system we must change the laws that helped to fuel the injustice -so my next step is political office. From generational trauma, pain and despair I've become a college graduate, community leader, a father, and future politician. We are not the sum of our past mistakes, we are the artist of the future we create. It's time to paint your own picture, one with your dreams right in the middle.

Made in the USA
Columbia, SC
01 March 2020